The Best
Small Towns
Under the Sun

Not bad for a day's catch. Fishing in Lake Lillian is reserved for children under 12 and seniors over 65.

The Best Small Towns Under the Sun

Robert J. Howard

Florida's Most Attractive— and Inviting—Little Communities

EPM
PUBLICATIONS, INC.

1003 Turkey Run Road   McLean, Virginia

Library of Congress Cataloging-in-Publication Data

Howard, Robert J.
  The best small towns under the sun: Florida's most attractive—and
inviting—little communities/Robert J. Howard.
     p.   cm.
  ISBN 0-939009-24-2
  1. Florida—Description and travel—1981—Guide-books.
2. Cities and towns—Florida—Guide-books.   I. Title.
F309.3.H67   1989
917.5904'63—dc20   89-11663
                                                                  CIP

Printed in the United States of America
EPM Publications, Inc. 1003 Turkey Run Road, McLean, Virginia 22101

Cover and book design by Tom Huestis
Color photographs courtesy of Florida
   Department of Commerce, Division of Tourism
Black/white photography by Robert J. Howard and Division of Tourism

CONTENTS

THE THIRTY-FIVE FINEST

Mention Florida to most people, and the places they usually think of first are Miami and Disney World. Still others think of Tampa, St. Petersburg, Jacksonville, Orlando or one of the other major cities of the state.

Florida to most is a world of sandy beaches, palm trees, sunshine, oranges and warm breezes. Tourists pour into the state by the millions each year, and many people come to stay. Some are retirees, determined to escape a cold climate for their remaining years. Still others are young people wanting to raise a family in a state that's been growing at a record pace ever since World War II. During the 1990s, Florida will become the fourth most populated state in the U.S., trailing only California, Texas and New York.

Florida, probably to the surprise of some, isn't all big cities, sandy beaches and palm trees. In this book you will be introduced to the state's small towns, most of which are unknown to many regular visitors and even some of the long-time residents.

There are 35 chapters, each devoted to a small town which I have personally visited and studied. Though I have lived in Florida since 1951 and served it as a newspaperman, I made extensive tours all over the state to get to know the smaller places better and to be able to select the very best.

All of the towns have a population under 15,000, and only one is more than 10,000. Three have populations of less than 1,000.

In arriving at the best 35, many factors were considered. Towns that simply didn't look good, and there are always some of these in any state, were immediately scratched off the list. If they looked good, then it was time to ask questions. The answers came from chamber of commerce officials, city managers, businessmen, people shopping in stores, retirees, young people and a general cross section who pointed out the pluses and minuses.

The questions dealt with recreational facilities, history, shopping availability, cultural activities, hospitals, libraries, real estate prices, cost of living, senior services, industries, educational facilities, employment opportunities, plans for the future and how people felt about their town.

Some towns, particularly the very small ones, didn't get a high rating in every category and even drew a blank in some, but they were such nice little places it would have been impossible not to include them.

Throughout the search it became increasingly apparent that many people had become disenchanted with Florida's large cities. Many people living in the small towns told of first moving to a Florida city, getting tired of the noise, the crime, the traffic congestion and the other negatives and transferring to towns where life moved at a slower pace.

In all the towns in this book there was a decided laid-back style of living. The residents got the job done, but they had time to visit with their neighbors, get involved in local activities and just plain relax.

Only a few towns in south Florida were selected, and this was largely due to the tremendous growth in that area. Small towns of a few years ago had either become cities or been absorbed by the major metropolitan areas.

There were only a few coastal towns that made the final list. Again, growth was the reason. Most new residents are attracted to either the Atlantic or the Gulf of Mexico, so many small towns along the coasts have left the small-town category.

There is no hesitation in recommending all 35 of these places to anyone shopping around for a small Florida town. Several more came close and may be included in any future listings a few years down the road. For now, though, these 35 were the best around.

R. J. H.

1. NORTHWEST (PANHANDLE)

Gulf Breeze

Population 7,000. Northwest. 6 miles from Pensacola, on gulf. White sand beaches. Long bridge connects town to Pensacola. Most growth since 60s. Good recreation center. Zoo, botanical gardens. Fishing, water sports big.

Florida's finest beaches are largely ignored by northern visitors and residents of the state except for those living in Florida's Panhandle. Because of this, the town of Gulf Breeze is relatively unknown by most Floridians. Both it and the beaches deserve a visit.

The beaches along Florida's upper gulf region are really something special. They stretch for more than 100 miles along the coast and are as white as sugar and almost as fine. Some visitors, at first glance, think they're looking at a newly fallen layer of snow. During the hot weather from May to September the beaches are crowded with area residents as well as thousands of visitors from other southern states. Otherwise, they are largely deserted but for the gulls, and other birds and an occasional beachcomber bent on getting away from it all for a quiet walk along this strand of white.

To be so close to this natural beauty on a permanent basis is the happy lot of more than 7,000 full-time residents of Gulf Breeze. Even when most of the state is cooking under the heat and humidity of a Florida summer, these fortunate folks are usually catching breezes drifting in from the gulf. Built on an east-west peninsula that juts into the gulf, the town has water on three sides and nothing to impede the flow of breezes.

H. Milo Stewart III

The perfect spot for tanning and catching gulf breezes, the sugar-white beaches of Gulf Breeze claim 343 days of sun a year.

Gulf Breeze is one of three incorporated towns in Santa Rosa County, the others being Milton and Jay. It's reached by a bridge of several miles across Pensacola Bay from Pensacola. Just a couple miles south of the peninsula and parallel to it is Santa Rosa Island, a very narrow strip of land that stretches for several miles and is designated as part of Escambia County. A bridge connects this island to Gulf Breeze, and the place is jammed with beachgoers on summer weekends.

In a popular song of the 30s, "Is It True What They Say About Dixie?" there's a line that asks, "Does the sun really shine all the time?" Phil Harris made it famous, and the writer must have had Gulf Breeze in mind. The sun here really does shine an average of 343 days of each year, so those who don't have a tan aren't really trying.

Even with all the sand, folks have managed to plant all kinds of grass, pretty flowers, a variety of shrubs and many trees. Along the beaches, sea oats have been planted, and that helps prevent erosion that could ruin this beautiful setting.

Though Gulf Breeze has been around for almost 60 years, it's only been a town of much consequence in the last three decades. When the bridge across Pensacola Bay was built back in 1931, there was a small hamlet here of a few people, but its name was Town Point. Even as late as 1940, the area around Gulf Breeze was swampy. There was a great deal of wildlife but few residents.

By 1950 the population had climbed to only 150, when two developers decided to make something of this place and started building. At that time there was nothing more than a hardware, a grocery and a service station. There had been a glue factory before World War II, but that was gone in 1950. Only some fishermen and a few commuters to Pensacola were living in Gulf Breeze.

The move by the developers paid off, and there were 500 people in town by 1961, when Gulf Breeze was incorporated. By 1980 there were 5,478.

For a town with such a short history, Gulf Breeze has fared surprisingly well. It's actually a complete community now with all the amenities that exist in towns with a far longer history. It has a complete school system, including a fine high school whose students have distinguished themselves with high scholastic scores.

With the gulf always within walking distance, the life-style here is naturally tied to the water. Nearly everyone spends considerable time outdoors, mostly boating, fishing and swimming. For those who don't favor sports, there's always the sun and the sand, and strolling along the beach. One man, who makes his living in Pensacola, claims that the beach is the best medicine he's found. He says, "I get back here after the daily rat race in Pensacola with my nerves jangling and my blood pressure up, and after 10 minutes walking along that beach I'm a new person. There's nothing like it."

For fishermen, there's a marina that can accommodate 20 boats in Gulf Breeze and five more marinas at Pensacola Beach on Santa Rosa Island. Twenty charter boats operate out of Gulf Breeze and 20 more in the area east of there. At Navarre Beach, just a few miles away, there is the world's longest fishing pier. Here surf-casters hook pompano, sheepshead, barracuda and redfish.

Forty-five percent of the city's acreage is devoted to playgrounds and parks. It has recently added a large recreation center equipped with a 10,000-square-foot gym, a 150-seat auditorium with stage, a large meeting room and kitchen. Outside this building are six lighted tennis courts, basketball courts for youths and adults, plus lighted softball, soccer and football fields. It's an impressive complex, thanks in no small measure to an active Gulf Breeze Sports Association that helps the city's recreation department.

Golf is also big in Gulf Breeze. The Tiger Point Golf Club, where Jerry Pate is the host pro, is a 48-hole layout and is the site of the Pensacola Open, a stop on the Professional Golf Association circuit each October. Holly By The Sea is an 18-hole course that's open to the public.

The town has had considerable recent publicity from three sources. The first is Colossus, the world's largest captive gorilla, which took up residence at the Zoo and Botanical Gardens in Gulf Breeze. Another source is the high school cheerleaders who won national titles. Also in the national news are the UFO sightings which started late in 1987 and are still going on, though less frequently. Some residents insist that what has been sighted are just airplanes from nearby Whiting Field, Eglin Air Force Base and Pensacola Naval Air Station. Others, slightly more vocal, insist they have seen strange-looking objects that don't have anything to do with airplanes or any other flying devices known to man. "I know what I've seen," one woman says, "and it definitely wasn't anything from this planet." Many pictures have been taken, but there have been no conclusions yet about what is going on up in the heavens.

The Zoo and Botanical Gardens, which opened in 1984, are the major tourist attraction in the area. Built on 20 acres of land along Gulf Breeze Parkway (U.S. Highway 98) they house some 400 exotic mammals, including lions, tigers, zebras, monkeys and giraffes. The animals live in open-air cages in beautifully landscaped gardens. Also on the site are a wildlife rehabilitation area and a sanctuary for birds maintained by the National Wildlife Rescue Sanctuary.

Colossus, quite naturally, is the most famous resident of the zoo. The gorilla weighs 600 pounds, stands six and a half feet tall and has a 92-inch arm span. He bunks in his choice of two climate-controlled living areas equipped with TV. Outside he has a 6,000 square-foot yard in which to roam. Recently the zoo acquired a mate for Colossus named Muke. She is the largest female gorilla in captivity, and zoo officials are quite excited about what may develop.

Living costs in Gulf Breeze, except for housing, are not much higher than in any other Florida town. Older homes are priced around $50,000, but the average home with three bedrooms and two baths costs between $100,000 and $150,000. Waterfront homes can run as much as $1 million to $2 million. The residential areas, particularly those with the more costly houses, are outstanding with plenty of trees and landscaped lawns and shrubs.

The less affluent have a wide selection of reasonably priced lots to choose from. The waterfront property, compared with such property in the rest of the country, is surprisingly affordable. There are some condos but not the number usually found in communities next to the gulf or ocean.

The oldest restored house in Jackson County is in historic Marianna, site of a Civil War skirmish.

The tax millage rates are $1.32 in the city and $10.37 in the county. (A tax millage rate is the amount charged on each $1,000 of assessed real estate. If, for example, a person owned a house assessed at $50,000 and the tax millage rate were $5 per $1,000, the owner would pay $250 in property tax.

The town has its own police department, a volunteer fire department, a large city hall, a 60-bed hospital and a good library open five days a week. Annual events include an arts and crafts show in late October, a watermelon festival and a King Neptune and Court Festival that starts in July 1989.

There's a good business district along the highway, including a new shopping center that is designed to resemble an old fishing village. Most residents commute to jobs in Pensacola or make their living off businesses that cater to the tourists as well as area residents. There are some small industries.

Growth here is not out of control, as evidenced by only 30 housing starts in 1988. Aside from some Canadian visitors in the winter, most residents live here year-round. It seems unlikely they will be deserting those white sand beaches.

Marianna

Population 7,000. In Panhandle, 75 miles west of Tallahassee. One of state's oldest towns. Several large industries. Community college. Large hospital, good library. Major crop is peanuts. State park, recreation areas nearby.

Back in the days before such major Florida cities as Miami, Fort Lauderdale, Orlando and Tampa even existed, Marianna was a thriving community in the state's Panhandle.

In the more than 160 years since Marianna was incorporated in 1828, this town has developed into one of the most prosperous spots in north Florida. It's a town with a great deal going for it and is considered an excellent place to live. The terrain is slightly rolling, and the white sand beaches of the Gulf of Mexico are less than an hour away.

Somewhat surprisingly this is an area of Florida that attracts few retirees. Marianna has made no effort to attract them but is quick to point out it definitely has no objections to their moving here. Concern over north Florida winters, which aren't really that bad, has kept many away, plus a feeling that the population, mostly native Southerners, would make it tough for a newcomer to be accepted. Though it's a little colder here than farther south, there have been only three light dustings of snow in the last 18 years, and the lowest temperature recorded during that time was 18 degrees. As far as being accepted, that's nonsense, according to local residents. "If they move here and get involved in the churches and local activities, they'll be accepted in a hurry," one man observed.

Marianna, the county seat of Jackson County, is one of the state's oldest towns, and the county is the third oldest in Florida. In July 1821, when Spain ceded Florida to the U.S., there were 54 pioneer families living in what is now Jackson County. The following year an act of the territorial legislature divided west Florida into two counties, Jackson and Escambia. Jackson then consisted of an area that has since been chopped up into 17 north Florida counties.

Marianna was founded as a rich man's town in 1827. During the competition with a place called Webbville over which town would become the county seat, an early settler commented, "In Webbville they serve whiskey from a jug, in Marianna from a bottle."

By 1830, the census of the county, named after Andrew Jackson, showed 3,907 residents. How Marianna got its name is still a mystery, though the favorite theory is that it was named after the wife of the town's founder, Robert Beveridge. The latter, a native of Scotland, had a beautiful wife named Anna Marie, and the supposition is that somebody reversed the names and came up with Marianna.

The town's major businesses face the public square, as they did when the town was first built. The stores and their owners have changed, but this square remains the center of activity.

Driving around the town for a few minutes gives visitors the immediate impression that Marianna is a prosperous place. The business section looks good, the streets are wide and clean, and the residential areas, with many brick homes, tell you that people who live here care about appearances. There are large shade trees up and down every street, well kept yards and many shrubs and flower gardens. The trees up here change colors in the fall and make Marianna look like a thousand other towns farther north.

The oldest restored house in the county, built in 1848, is now occupied by the chamber of commerce, but there are dozens of other homes around town from the 19th century. Many are antebellum.

Marianna's population is now about 7,000 and has been largely unchanged for the last 25 years. The county population is 43,000 and is expected to reach 50,000 by 2000. About 14.7 percent of the residents are over 65.

There will be some growth in Marianna if it pushes water and sewer service across the Chipola River, its eastern boundary, but this is about 10 years away.

Jackson County is the only one in Florida bordered by both Alabama and Georgia. Some Marianna businessmen, on trips outside the southeast, like to tell people they're from L. A.

When the eyes roll at that southern accent, they quickly explain that the L.A. means Lower Alabama.

The employment picture in Marianna is excellent, thanks to several thriving industries and three institutions in the immediate area. For the last 10 years the unemployment rate has been about six percent. While there are some small industries, the bigger ones are the Russell Corp., maker of sportswear, with 500 employees; Lehigh Furniture, 435 employees; Unimac, a washing machine manufacturer with 275 employees, and Stone Container Corp., a lumber firm with 152 employees.

The institutions include a federal prison that has 500 employees, the Arthur G. Dozier School for delinquent teenagers with 600 employees, and the Sunland Training Center, occupied mostly by mentally retarded adults, which also employs 600.

Most of Marianna's growth has been just outside the city, resulting in the addition of a shopping center in 1989 of 130,000 square feet. Two more are planned for later.

There's plenty of good fishing in the area, but none better than Merritt's Mill Pond just east of town—18 miles long and well known for five state record catches of shellcrackers since 1979. It's near the headwaters of Blue Springs, which pump 123 million gallons of fresh water every day into the mill pond from an underwater cave. Hunting for deer and small game is also good in the area.

Just a couple miles north of Marianna is Florida Caverns State Park, opened in 1942 and a great place for swimming, fishing, canoeing and camping. Other good outdoor locations are at Three Rivers State Recreation Area, east of town, and Blue Springs Recreation Area, where there are slides, diving boards and bathhouses. A nine-hole golf course is near Florida Caverns. Wooded areas surround Marianna with 20 miles of nature trails for jogging and walking.

A World War II air base is now being utilized as the Marianna airport with two 5,000-foot runways. A good recreation complex has been developed here that includes the high school football stadium and four baseball fields for use by

Pony Leagues and others. Nearby are 900 acres set aside for an industrial park.

Chipola Junior College, started in 1947, and the third oldest junior college in Florida, is located a few blocks north of the downtown area. It has 2,000 students on a large wooded campus that has plenty of room to grow. A new fieldhouse was recently built there, the old one having been converted into an auditorium for the presentation of little theater plays and other cultural events. Six tennis courts and four racquetball courts at the college are also available for use by the public. Chipola has the highest percentage of graduates going on to four-year schools of any junior college in the state.

A large National Guard Armory is used heavily for meetings and various public functions. Also near downtown are a very adequate library with 30,000 volumes and Jackson Hospital, a modern facility of 107 beds. In an unusual arrangement, the town owns two nursing homes that have 250 rooms.

In the farming community outside town, nothing is bigger than peanuts. Jackson County produces 82 percent of all the peanuts raised in Florida, and that's thousands of tons. Soybeans and corn are next in importance, followed by beef cattle raising.

Despite all it has going for it now, Marianna doesn't forget its past, and foremost in this is the Battle of Marianna. Largely ignored by most historians, this battle was really more of a skirmish. On September 27, 1864 a force of Union cavalry and mounted infantry approached Marianna after camping northeast of there the night before. This was in the late stages of the Civil War, and only older men and boys under 16, armed with squirrel rifles and old guns, were left to defend Marianna. The Union had three battalions of 900 men, so it was no match.

After the Union troops burned a church and five defenders inside it, the battle finally ended. Two Union officers were killed and 32 men wounded, while the Marianna defenders had 10 killed and 15 wounded.

The burned church was St. Luke's Episcopal. The pulpit Bible, saved by a Union officer from the fire, is on display in a glass case in the present church. Buried in the adjoining churchyard are John Milton, the governor of Florida during the Civil War, and many witnesses to the event of 1864.

Before the war, wealthy planters in the area, all conservatives, had opposed secession, but the county supported the Confederacy and opposed the rule of the carpetbaggers that followed the war.

Good houses are not expensive in Marianna. Brick homes with three bedrooms and two baths on an acre lot will run from $80,000 to $95,000. Most mobile homes are outside the city. The tax millage rate in Marianna is only $1.74 while the county rate is $13.23.

There are good prospects for attracting several more industries. The good life-style here and the quality of the labor force have helped greatly in this effort.

Few Florida towns have such a long history. For now, though, Marianna seems more intent on concentrating on the future, and that can only be described as bright.

Milton

Population 7,500. Northwest. 10 miles northeast of Pensacola. Near three large military bases. Restored opera house, hotel. Top cotton producing county in state.

For a town that started out with the somewhat ignominious name of Scratch Ankle, Milton has come a long way and is now one of the foremost places in Florida's Panhandle.

Located in the northwest corner of the state between Pensacola and Fort Walton Beach, Milton has been around since 1825, when a trading post was established there. The area was infested with briers, so the name of Scratch Ankle didn't seem inappropriate at the time. In the years since, the town has become the county seat of Santa Rosa County, acquired a population of 7,500 and is a very desirable place to live. Named after John Milton, the governor of Florida during the Civil War, Milton is a town that has a great many pluses, as does much of the county in which it's located.

Like so many of Florida's coastal areas, the country around Milton came under the Spanish influence in the 16th century. A Spanish conquistador, Don Tristan de Luna, explored the area in 1559, and the lower bay below Milton is still called Santa Maria de Galvez, a name given it by de Luna.

Two large military bases, Whiting Field and Eglin Air Force Base, have contributed greatly to the growth of Milton. Whiting Field, a naval base for training helicopter pilots, is seven miles north of Milton, while the air force base is in the southeast corner of the county. Impressed with the life-style in Milton, many men who have been stationed at these two bases have settled there when they retired.

Whiting, which is also a primary training base, plays a large role in Milton's economy. In addition to the 1,400 men stationed at the base, 3,100 civilian employees work there.

Milton residents are used to the sounds of airplanes. Whiting is second only to O'Hare Field in Chicago in the number of takeoffs and landings, while Eglin and nearby Pensacola Naval Air Station also send many planes zooming through the skies on a daily basis.

An active historical group and a city administration that takes pride in its town have combined to help make Milton such an outstanding location. The Santa Rosa Historical Society, with 150 members, has been responsible for two recent major renovation projects, the Imogene Theater and the adjoining town of Bagdad.

The Imogene, an opera house built in 1913 and restored in 1985 by the society, is an impressive building with three-brick-thick walls and eight-foot high windows. Offices and a local museum are on the first floor, while the upstairs is devoted to concerts, little theater plays, movies, ballroom dancing, meetings, proms and parties. The building is a Milton showplace.

In Bagdad, a lumber mill town from the 1820s until the 1930s, another outstanding job of restoration has been accomplished. Dozens of mills made Bagdad a lumber center in the early years, but the last mill closed in 1937, and the town slipped into a long period of decline. The society became active in restoring the town, and now it's a quaint little historic village with dozens of restored Victorian houses that seem to sparkle in the sun with all their new coats of paint and repairs.

Across the street from the opera house is another great work of restoration—the Exchange Hotel. Built as a telephone exchange in 1912, it later became a hotel for several years, then was abandoned. An eyesore for a long period, it was taken over by a local businessman in 1981 and restored for a bed and breakfast spot in 1983. During its earlier days as a hotel, baseball Hall of Famer Ted Williams stayed there while serving as a World War II flight instructor at nearby Whiting Field.

The city also has played a major role in improving the downtown area near the hotel and opera house. To the east just over the bridge across Blackwater River the city built an attractive Riverwalk Park. The city docks were located here in the early days, but now there's a charming gazebo and a winding boardwalk along the river on both sides of U.S. Highway 90. Dedicated in 1987, it is easily accessible by water through docking facilities. With that opera house and hotel in the background, the boardwalk looks like it's offering a stroll into history.

The city takes great pride in its appearance and has reduced the litter picked up by its trucks by 91 percent in the last five years. Residents also enjoy the second lowest gas rate in the state since the city owns its own gas works.

Living costs in Milton are very reasonable. The average price of a home is about $42,000, and a three-bedroom, two-bath home is usually priced around $50,000. New homes are being built at a steady pace. Milton's tax millage rate is only $1.68, while the county rate is $10.37.

The county's population is about 65,000, so there's plenty of room left for growth. About two-thirds of the county is in forest, including the Blackwater River State Forest of 183,000 acres, 15 miles north of Milton and the largest state forest in Florida. There are no more virgin forests left, but this second growth of cypress, juniper and pine offers great hiking, camping, horseback riding and hunting.

At the southern end of the forest is Blackwater River State Park, located directly on the river. The water is free of pollution and ideal for swimming, fishing and canoeing. In the wooded areas are white-tailed deer, bobcats and turkeys.

With the Blackwater River as well as the Coldwater, Sweetwater and Juniper rivers available nearby, Milton has been designated by the state as the canoe capital of Florida. The rivers furnish a trail winding 100 miles from the Alabama line to Blackwater Bay, and canoeing enthusiasts from all parts of Florida as well as other southeastern states are drawn here by the crystal clear water.

Recreational facilities are plentiful in Milton. In addition to four lighted tennis courts, basketball courts and a baseball field at a city park, soccer fields, two girls baseball fields and an exercise trail at a branch of Pensacola Junior College are available to the public. Handball and volleyball facilities are planned. Milton High School boasts extensive facilities for sports and an impressive football stadium.

Plans call for converting abandoned railroad tracks in town to a biking and jogging path. Three golf courses are in the immediate area.

Even with so much of the county occupied by forests and the bases, there's still room for agriculture, and Santa Rosa has become the top cotton-producing county in the state harvesting over 20,000 bales annually. It also produces large quantities of peanuts.

Several major industries contribute greatly to a healthy economic climate in Milton. These include American Cyanamid, makers of acrylic fiber, with 325 employees; Russell Corp., a sportswear manufacturer with 220 employees; Vanity Fair Mills, a lingerie company employing 520, and Baja Boats, a motor cruiser firm with 400 employees. The unemployment rate is understandably low at 5.9 percent.

An Industrial Development Authority, interested in attracting even more industries, is located in the old L&N depot. Built in 1909 and returned to its original condition, including a red tile roof, it also serves as headquarters for that busy historical society and the Santa Rosa Art Association, which uses the building for workshops and meetings.

Well preserved old houses are common throughout Milton's

residential sections. The oldest documented house is the McDougal House, built before 1866. St. Mary's Episcopal Church, dating back to 1878, is the oldest non-residential building. Magnolia, live oak and pecan trees line the streets and azaleas, camelias and dogwoods abound in the yards.

There are many special events on the schedule each year, including the Scratch Ankle Spring Festival in March, the Blackwater Heritage Tour of the historic areas in December, Depot Day and an accompanying arts and crafts show in November and a big July 4th Riverfest. Still other events are the world's largest tube float, a fishing tournament, bathtub races, a canoe caravan and a few more art shows.

On the education front, Milton has had an outstanding vocational-technical center since 1982, offering training programs based on the needs of the area, and the branch of Pensacola Junior College located on a wooded campus on the edge of town. The University of West Florida, a four-year school, is only 14 miles away in Pensacola. Adult education courses are offered at the high school and the vocational school.

Medical facilities are ample with the Santa Rosa Medical Center of 152 beds.

Milton's other assets include a large library with 34,000 volumes, a civic center and a senior center that serves 300 people in the county and has a van for transporting seniors for shopping and doctor appointments.

The county extends from the Alabama line on the north to the Gulf of Mexico and its white sand beaches to the south, just 25 miles from Milton. Since 1980 the population growth in the county has been 19 percent. The median age is 27.8 and only 20 percent of the population are over 50.

Milton can best be described as a town that has about everything going for it. It has all the amenities, an excellent quality of life, a thriving economy, people who are proud of their town and want to make it even better, ready access to forests and streams and sandy beaches and an air of optimism that hits you as soon as you cross the Blackwater River into the town.

Silver-domed courthouse in Monticello, patterned after Thomas Jefferson's home in Virginia.

Live Oak

Population 7,603. North. Near Panhandle, close to Georgia, just off I-10. Suwannee River borders county on three sides. Poultry, tobacco main industries. Large library, good museum. Hospital. Two state parks in county.

No county in Florida is more aptly named than Suwannee. Located in north central Florida, only a few miles from Georgia, the county is bordered on three sides by the historic Suwannee River.

Folks up in this part of the state, just a short ways from where the Panhandle begins, have a great fondness for the Suwannee. Made famous by a Stephen Foster song, this river is one of the prettiest in Dixie. It flows out of Georgia and winds its way through the wooded landscape of north Florida before entering the Gulf of Mexico about 40 miles south of Suwannee County.

The Suwannee County seat is Live Oak, a town named for one of Florida's most common trees. Usually bedecked with strands of Spanish moss, the live oak grows to great proportions and is noted for its longevity. Many are well over a century old. According to local historians, section hands on the Seaboard Railroad gave Live Oak its name. They would sweat under a blazing sun, then seek some shade under the same tree every day while eating their lunch. "It's about time to eat," one of them is supposed to have said, "let's go to the big live oak." The town grew up around the tree.

Live Oak is a prosperous community in an area where agriculture plays an important role in the scheme of things. It's also a town with a modernized business district spread over several blocks and attractive residential areas with many brick homes, well-tended lawns and, of course, many live oak trees. It's a town where visitors feel comfortable almost immediately. Folks smile and take a justified pride in their community. People don't seem to be in a mad dash, but they manage to accomplish a great deal.

Poultry and tobacco are the major business commodities around Live Oak. In the area 100 farmers have contracts with Gold Kist to raise chickens. The Gold Kist poultry plant, 12 miles from Live Oak, employs 575 people and processes 650,000 chickens every week. That figures out to 1,300,000 drumsticks.

Tobacco, despite all the adverse publicity about smoking, still is a major industry. The amount raised is almost as much as in earlier days when the tobacco auction was the biggest event of the year. There were 300 families producing the crop in the years before World War II, but this figure is down to fewer than 50 families now. It's flue-cured tobacco used for cigarettes, and its production accounts for a third of the farm labor market in the Live Oak area. Only in Live Oak and the neighboring towns of Lake City and Madison is tobacco a major crop. The auctions are still held every summer.

Just off Interstate 10, and with Interstate 75 only 20 miles east of the town, Live Oak is well located from a transportation standpoint. It's one hour from here to Gainesville, home of the state university, and about 90 minutes to Jacksonville and the state capital in Tallahassee. Area residents can reach the Jacksonville International Airport in the same time as people living in Jacksonville suburbs on the other side of the city from the airport.

The latest population figure for Live Oak is 7,603. There was a 42 percent increase in the county's growth in the 70s, and in Live Oak there has been an 18 percent increase since 1980. Projections call for a county population of 32,000 by 2000, which would be a healthy growth from the 22,287 in 1980.

Unlike most Florida counties farther south in the peninsula, where development was slow until late in the 19th century, Suwannee County and Live Oak got a much earlier start. The county was created in 1858, and the 1860 census listed the population as 1,467 whites and 835 slaves. Live Oak got its first post office in 1866, and the town became the county seat in 1875. It was incorporated three years later.

By 1900 only six houses in Live Oak had bathroom fixtures, and the main street didn't get paved until 1913. The impressive courthouse in the middle of town was built in 1918, nine years after the Union depot was constructed. The depot is now boarded up, but may become a branch of North Florida Junior College in Madison.

An outstanding museum is now located over the police station but will soon be moved to a renovated 1903 railroad freight station. The exhibits feature extensive memorabilia from bygone eras, including an authentic moonshine still, a restored Timucuan Indian village that was done by a local high school group, and a Pioneer Room showing how the early settlers lived in the 1870s.

In addition to those working in the poultry and tobacco industries, quite a few Live Oak residents commute to jobs outside the county, some to Lake City and others to the phosphate mining operations in neighboring Hamilton County.

There are two large complexes outside Live Oak that also provide employment. The Advent Christian Village on the Suwannee River, which employs about 300 people, is a haven for homeless and abused children as well as many retirees. The Florida Sheriff's Boys Ranch, for about 100 boys from all parts of the state, is 12 miles from Live Oak and employs another 130.

In the farm land surrounding Live Oak, watermelons are a major crop, and there are 20 dairies in the county, double that of just 10 years ago. A multi-million dollar farmers market operates in the county and sells to brokers and the retail trade.

Amenities are well covered, and the recreational needs of the community are not neglected. The Suwannee River, just 10 miles from town, is popular for swimming, canoeing, boating and fishing. Several fresh water springs in the area, always at 72 degrees, are excellent for swimming.

In town, a large recreation area has lighted tennis and racquetball courts, a softball field, a Little League field and playground equipment. Nearby is a public swimming pool. Golfers have a choice between a 9-hole course in Live Oak and 18-hole courses in Lake City and Valdosta, GA.

There are two nice state parks in the county, the Suwannee River State Park in the northwest corner, and Ichetucknee Springs in the southeast corner. The latter is popular for tubing and scuba diving.

The town's health needs are handled by the Suwannee Hospital, a 60-bed facility that opened in 1948. A new hospital, also with 60 beds, and a senior center are scheduled for the near future.

An attractive library next to the courthouse houses 28,000 volumes. It serves a six-county area and is the headquarters for the Suwannee River Regional Library System.

There are two-year colleges in both Lake City and Madison. The latter offers night classes in the local high school, and a vocational school is in a separate building near the high school. Local residents point with pride to the fact that the academic team from the high school has won state championships in two of the last three years.

An active Artists Guild in Live Oak promotes the visual arts with an annual art show, and a Suwannee Valley little theater group stages several productions annually. The biggest event of the year is Christmas on the Suwannee, held the first weekend in December and attracting 10,000 people to an arts and crafts show, entertainment around the courthouse and a Christmas parade at night. Continuing a 75-year-old tradition, the Suwannee County Fair, Florida's oldest, takes place in October.

Anyone looking for a home here can purchase a good three-bedroom, two-bath home for $50,000. There are three mobile home parks in town and three more just outside. The millage rates are $5.97 in the city and $16.97 in the county.

For shopping, there are three large centers and a good selection of stores in the downtown area.

It's been 450 years since Hernando de Soto crossed the Suwannee River a few miles west of Live Oak on his expedition to bring the Spanish-owned region of Florida under control. His mission failed, as everyone knows. Long under local control, the area continues to prosper. The folks in Live Oak will attest to that.

Madison

Population 3,700. North. 50 miles east of Tallahassee, near Georgia line. Tobacco is major crop. Large meat-packing plant. Few retirees. New library. Community college. Many antebellum homes. Historic town.

Strolling through many streets of Madison is almost like a return to the 19th century. Unquestionably one of the prettiest towns in Florida, Madison was settled well before the Civil War and has managed to preserve many of the buildings from that era.

Madison is a typical small town of the Deep South. It's the county seat of Madison County, and its northern border is the Georgia state line. The courthouse is in the middle of town with the business district surrounding it. The customary Confederate monument stands across the street in a neat city park. And spreading out from all this are block after block of white columned homes from the last century along streets lined with giant live oak trees.

In the park with the Confederate monument is another noting that Colin Kelly, the first U.S. hero and Medal of Honor winner of World War II, was a native of Madison. Almost 50 years later his name is still remembered for his great daring in those grim weeks after Pearl Harbor.

Madison's history goes back to 1838, when cotton planters from South Carolina settled the town, though there were residents in the county even before that. The county was established in 1827, and a census in 1830 showed there were 259 whites and 263 slaves.

By 1850 the county population had grown to more than 5,000 people, and cotton had already become the major crop.

A center for the cotton industry in the 1800s, Madison maintains the antebellum aura of a small town in the Deep South.

There were more than 200,000 acres of sea-island cotton in Florida by the 1870s, and Madison was one of the centers of the industry. The world's largest long-leaf cotton gin was located in Madison, before the boll weevil arrived in 1916 and just about wiped out all the cotton in Florida and most other areas of Dixie.

With cotton's demise, Madison turned to other ventures and now boasts a widely diversified economy. The county produces a variety of crops, and Madison has an industrial park of 602 acres that provides the base for hundreds of jobs.

A meat packing subsidiary of the Winn Dixie grocery chain has nearly 550 employees, and ITT operates a metal products plant that employs another 250. A firm that prints business cards has 125 employees.

On the agricultural front, tobacco is the number one crop. It's flue-cured tobacco used in making cigarettes, and at one time 1,100 growers produced it. The number is now down to 25, but the total acreage is about the same and the tobacco auctions still are held in the late summer.

Gone from the scene is the shade tobacco used in cigar wrappers. There were six to eight large growers here, and their product was considered an aristocracy crop. Then Castro took over Cuba, and the research and seeds of the cigar industry went to Central America about 15 years ago.

Watermelons also are a major crop, and considerable acreage is devoted to corn, soybeans, peaches and the raising of cattle, hogs and chickens.

Many tree farms of pines and hardwood can be seen in Madison County. It takes almost 20 years to raise a crop of trees. Then they are harvested and replanted. A total of 72 firms here engage in pulpwood and other timber-related activities.

Living costs in Madison are among the lowest in Florida. Most of the 250 employees at the new medium security prison here will earn an average starting salary of $16,000 to $17,000 and, as a chamber of commerce executive points out, "That's good money around here."

There were virtually no retirees moving into Madison until about 10 years ago. Now they are discovering this little town and transferring here from the larger cities in south Florida. A social caste system that had existed well into this century has now disappeared, and outsiders find no trouble being assimilated into the Madison life-style.

A different kind of outsider moved in during 1988—moviemakers from Orlando, producing a movie named "The Spring." It was Madison's first exposure to this industry, and many residents enjoyed working as extras in the filming.

All the news in recent years hasn't been good. A deadly tornado cut an 18-mile swath across Madison County in 1988, killing four persons and doing $4 million in damage to the North Florida Junior College in Madison. The rest of the town escaped all but a little damage, and the college, which has already replaced everything except the auditorium, will be completely rebuilt within a couple of years.

The courthouse, with its impressive silver dome, looms over everything in Madison. Built in 1914, it is the third courthouse the county has had. Two earlier ones were destroyed by fires; the first was the site of a convention in 1845 that nominated Florida's first governor under statehood.

This courthouse made news in 1988 when a renovation project was completed and the courtroom restored to look as it did in its earliest days. Air conditioning was added, however, so the windows could be closed during court sessions. Now the birds don't fly through the open windows as they did previously, and court doesn't have to suspend procedures when big trucks rumble by on Highway 90.

Madison is full of historic structures. The oldest house in town, still occupied, was built in 1849, and a small wooden Episcopal church, built in 1843, still stands. Just down the street from the courthouse is the Wardlaw-Smith house, a stately mansion of Greek Revival architecture that dates from 1860. It's been well preserved and is now open to the public. In 1864 the house served as a Confederate hospital after the Battle of Olustee, the only Civil War battle fought on Florida soil. Behind the house grows a live oak that's huge even by north Florida standards. Planted in 1830, it has a spread of 144 feet, a circumference of 19 feet, four inches, and is 83 feet high.

Memories of the golden years when cotton was king are preserved in a little park near the railroad. A small patch of cotton grows there next to the 16-foot drive wheel for a 500-horsepower engine that once pulled 65 gins in the world's largest cotton processing plant.

Despite all the history here, Madison is a very modern town that boasts more amenities than most towns of only 3,700 population. There's an attractive business district around the courthouse, and a new shopping center is planned.

Madison County Memorial Hospital has 54 beds and serves all of the county. There also are major hospitals nearby in Valdosta, Georgia and Tallahassee.

A new library will soon open, replacing another new one leveled by the 1988 tornado. Fortunately, the books hadn't been moved in yet.

There's a good variety of recreation available in the area. A city recreation park has four softball fields and a Little League field. The junior college has several tennis courts that are used by the public, and there is an 18-hole golf course in Madison. Bass fishing is excellent at Cherry Lake, a few miles north of town, and the Suwannee, Aucilla and Withlacoochee Rivers are good for pan fishing as well as bass. Lake Francis, right near the middle of town, is fished regularly for pan fish.

The Suwannee and Withlacoochee are designated canoe trails, and both are used for swimming, as are the many natural springs in the county that produce crystal clear water at a constant 72 degrees.

Vast timber lands in the county are used for hunting deer, small game, doves and quail, and a permit to hunt on most lands costs only $5. The area has several hunting clubs and lodges.

The junior college plays a major role in the life of Madison. Adult education classes are offered there, and local residents take part in plays and other productions at the school. An artists program will be revived when the new auditorium opens.

An active senior center near downtown has a Meals on Wheels program, homemaking services, crafts lessons in ceramics, quilting and crocheting and computer literacy classes. The center serves 500 and even provides transportation to doctors appointments.

The biggest event of the year is Downhome Days in April. This includes an arts and crafts festival, entertainment downtown and a rodeo at the Ag Center.

Complete restoration of the downtown is planned to make the town look as it did in 1914. The plans call for brick sidewalks, utilities underground, benches and shrubs over a 10-block area. There are no plans for any major population influx. The census count in 1980 was 14,894 in the county, and this is supposed to reach only 16,500 by 2000.

In Madison, housing costs are not high. A new three-bedroom, two-bath home can be built for $50,000. The millage rate is between $4 and $5 in town and about $15 in the county.

Madison is a town that has done a terrific job in preserving its past while concentrating on the present. There's a good mix of agriculture and industry. The life-style is definitely uncomplicated, and new residents are well pleased they made the move here.

Monticello

Population 3,000. North. 25 miles east of Tallahassee, near Georgia and gulf. Courthouse modeled after Jefferson's home (see p. 24). Outstanding restored opera house. Several small industries. Over 40 19th-century buildings. Large library, hospital.

Of all the Florida towns that have made an effort to preserve their past, none has done a better job than Monticello.

This north Florida town, 23 miles east of Tallahassee and with a population of 3,000, has an historic district listed in the National Register of Historic Places that contains over 40 buildings dating back to the 19th century. Many of the houses are antebellum, and most of the commercial buildings are from the last quarter of the 19th century. The town is largely intact from the last century, more so than almost any town in the state, and the buildings offer a fine example of Greek Revival, Classic Revival and Stick Style architecture.

Monticello is a town you fall in love with as soon as you catch a glimpse of that courthouse, which dominates the scene as you approach the town from any direction. Built in 1909 on the exact site of the original 1835 structure, this courthouse is in the middle of town. All the roads coming into town circle the courthouse and the streets radiate from it.

Thomas Jefferson had a great impact on Monticello and the county in which it's located. The town's original name in 1826 had been Robison, then Jefferson Courthouse after the county, named for Jefferson, was formed in 1827. After Jefferson died in July 1826, the residents decided to name the town Monticello after his home in Virginia. The courthouse, patterned after Monticello, is a charming little building with a silver dome. It cost only $40,000 to build, but it's the most eye-catching structure in town.

Like most north Florida towns, Monticello has a long history. Apalachee Indians were the original settlers, and in the area where Jefferson County is now Spanish missions, long since gone, were scattered across the landscape. The first white man to visit this area was Panfilo de Harvaez, who landed on the gulf coast in 1528. Just 11 years later Hernando de Soto came through in his long and extensive explorations of Florida. As late as 1822, Pensacola and St. Augustine were the only existing towns in the state. Peninsula Florida was a vast wilderness.

The first white visitors to stay in the present Jefferson County came from the seaboard states of the U.S. and were mainly interested in raising cotton. They found they could raise superior cotton in the red clay hills of this middle north Florida county. By 1830 the county's first census showed there were 3,314 residents—1,695 free white, 1,612 slaves and 7 free Negroes.

At the time the Civil War erupted in 1861 Monticello was firm in opposing the abolition of slavery and took a leading role in Florida's secession from the Union.

There were grim days after the war ended. The carpetbaggers moved in and hard times delayed further building in Monticello until the end of Reconstruction in the 1880s. Fires after the war destroyed most of the early business buildings, but many of the houses survived and are still here.

An interesting self-guided walking tour, with 28 stops at older houses, businesses and other landmarks of the town, is well worth the time. The chamber of commerce, located in a former Catholic church, gives out brochures explaining the tour stops. Highlights include the Wirick-Simmons House, built in 1833 and the headquarters of the Jefferson County Historical Society; the Methodist, Episcopal and Presbyterian churches, each with stained glass windows from the last century; the old cemetery, dating back to 1827 and containing the graves of people born in the 18th century plus both Confederate and Union soldiers, and the Avenue of Oaks, a natural cathedral of live oaks planted in 1889 and a breathtaking sight.

One of the most noteworthy restoration efforts in the state has been going on in recent years directly across the street from the courthouse—the Perkins Opera House, built in 1890. A remarkable structure for the time, it seated 600, had the largest stage in the entire southeast and made Monticello the cultural center of north Florida.

In the years that followed, the fortunes of the opera house declined and by the 1930s it was being used as a movie theater. That folded in the Great Depression, and the building was occupied mostly by stores. By the late 1960s, the Perkins was threatened with demolition for the building of a gas station. Local residents came to the rescue at this point, and the restoration was begun in the early 70s. With $528,000 in donations and a state grant, the Perkins gradually has been restored to the glory of its earliest days. The project is to be completed in time to celebrate the building's centennial in 1990.

Ceilings are 16 feet high, and the acoustics have been labeled by experts as perfect, as is the line of sight from the original building. Viewing from all seats is unobstructed. Overhead are three original gas chandeliers. The floors remain from 1890, and the only major change has been the building of an impressive staircase from the ground floor where attractive shops will be located.

The balcony, which was used for the black residents in the early days with their own entrance and stairway on the side, also remains intact. An overzealous workman was about to smooth out some initials that had been carved long ago in the railing of the balcony when a preservationist caught him in time, and the carvings survived.

Even some of the original seats remain, complete with metal racks underneath for the hats of gentlemen patrons. Missing is the pot bellied stove that heated the place.

An opera is scheduled before the opening with the Florida State University orchestra performing. Road shows, garden club and fashion shows, ballet productions, one-man intimate shows and performances by the Monticello Players will take place throughout the year.

Jefferson County, with a population of 12,500, has the distinction of being the only county in Florida that stretches from the Georgia border to the Gulf of Mexico. Monticello is the county's only incorporated town and the center of most activity. The town's largest employer is Command Enterprises, a company that makes aprons and smocks for Sears and K-Mart and employs 250 people. More than 500 are employed by other firms involved in manufacturing cellulose insulation and precision tools as well as by a smelting plant, large nursery stock operations and dairy related industries. The county's Economic Development Corp. owns a 15-acre tract just south of Monticello. Many residents commute to jobs in state government at the capital in Tallahassee.

Watermelons are the most popular crop in the county, followed by pecans, peanuts, cotton and corn. More than a third of all pecan trees in the U.S. grow here. Berry pickers get plenty of exercise with a choice of strawberries, blueberries and raspberries.

There's good fishing in Lake Miccosukee, eight miles away, and plenty of hunting in the surrounding wooded areas. Deer, small game and birds are hunted, though permission is needed from the land owners, which reportedly is not difficult to arrange.

A Jefferson County recreation park on the edge of town has four tennis courts, softball and Little League fields and a handball court. There's a nine-hole golf course and swimming pool at the Monticello Country Club.

The town has a health clinic, but the nearest hospitals are in Thomasville, Georgia and Tallahassee. A helicopter can lift patients to the Tallahassee hospitals in minutes.

Though only 13.6 percent of the population are over 65, Monticello has been attracting retirees from the west coast of Florida and south Florida. One lady, a native of Brooklyn, moved here from a town in New York and loves it. With Tallahassee so close, the residents have plenty of opportunities to attend the various performances by the symphony orchestra and civic ballet groups there as well as concerts and sports events in the Tallahassee Civic Center, art galleries and museums.

Monticello moved its 17,000 volume library into attractive quarters in a renovated building in 1987.

The terrain around Monticello is mostly rolling, and the elevation is 235 feet, which is high by Florida standards. Outside the town are several plantations, including one owned by media and sports magnate Ted Turner.

There's a good variety of real estate offerings. A recent listing showed a used two-bedroom home on a city street for

Alachua calls itself the Good Life Community. Above, pleasant residential sections spread out from historic Main Street.

$35,000, another with three acres, three bedrooms, two baths, a big kitchen and a yard full of dogwoods for $64,900 and still another with three bedrooms and two baths on a spring-fed creek for $69,500. For the affluent there was a country estate with vaulted ceiling on 10 acres for $250,000. The millage rates are $8.5 in the city and $13.09 in the county.

A recent addition to the local scene has been the Jefferson Kennel Club, a dog racing track three miles outside the town operating three months during the summer.

Visitors to Monticello in the fall from the southern parts of Florida marvel at the changing colors of the leaves. The most spectacular are the maples, popcorns and dogwoods. The latter two turn a brilliant red and almost cover the town.

Despite all the history here and the old buildings, Monticello is not a town living in the past. While it's justifiably proud of its heritage, there's a good balance of the old and the new. Like most other north Florida towns, it hasn't experienced any large-scale growth. Projections call for only 15,700 people in Jefferson County by 2010.

3. NORTH CENTRAL

Alachua

Population 4,500. Expect 25,000 by 2000. North Central. 14 miles north of Gainesville on I-75. 3 major industries. Variety of crops. 30 square miles in size. Close to state university, community college.

For many years it was just another small town 14 miles northwest of the University of Florida in Gainesville. In recent years, though, Alachua has begun to flex its muscles and become a bustling place with high ambitions for the immediate future.

The population of Alachua, (pronounced A-lá-Chewa), exploded to a hefty 4,500 in the late 1980s, and city planners project 25,000 by 2000.

If the projections are reached, Alachua will have deserted the small town category. It seems quite likely that will happen, given its 30 square miles of space. The town expanded its city limits recently from five square miles to 30, making it only slightly smaller than Gainesville in size. Gainesville's population of 88,000 includes about 35,000 students at the university.

In its early days, Alachua was the county seat of Alachua County, though it was called Newnansville then. The town wasn't platted until the 1890s, and growth through the early years was slow.

The area around here is rich in history. Over a century ago Queen Victoria, Prince Albert and their party reportedly traveled through an area a few miles from Alachua in wagons. The Bellamy Road, one of Florida's most famous highways, passes just six miles northwest of town. A part of the 350-mile road that ran all the way across the top of the state from Pensacola to St. Augustine, it was built, after approval from Congress, by John Bellamy in the 1820s. Explored in the 16th century by Hernando de Soto and formerly home to Timucuan Indians, most of this portion of Florida was a jungle when construction began. Clearing millions of trees and thick underbrush to build such a road was a mighty achievement. The road was 15 to 21 feet wide, and its length was measured by counting the revolutions of an ox-cart wheel. Bellamy Road is still here and being used, but to most residents it's just another side road, cut in two pieces when Interstate 75 was constructed in the 1950s.

Despite being at the point where Interstate 75 and busy U.S. Highway 441 intersect, Alachua is still largely rural. Farming in the surrounding area is big business. As in other counties west of here, tobacco is a major crop and pumps several million dollars into the economy each year. In addition, corn, soybeans, watermelons and vegetables are considered important crops. The county is also into cattle raising on a big scale, and the Santa Fe Ranch is noted for having the largest herd of Herefords in the southeast. In recent years, grapes, blueberries and apples also have been produced.

Alachua, which is an Indian word meaning jug, calls itself "The Good Life Community." The title is not a misnomer. The town has two business districts. The original one was built down the center of the town on what was called the Dixie Highway. This is now known as Historic Main Street. When U.S. 441 was built in 1936, another business district started springing up there, and now the shopping centers, fast food restaurants and other businesses are concentrated on that road. Historic Main street is still operating and will be restored to its original appearance with new store fronts, underground utilities, brick sidewalks and benches, all to be completed through the use of private funds.

Unemployment in Alachua is only 3.5 percent, and it's not expected to climb. There are three major industries in town, led by Gates Batteries, producers of rechargeable batteries for everything from flashlights to jet airplanes. This company employs 950 people and is followed by Hunter Marine, manufacturer of fine boats and employer of another 320. The third company is Driltech, a firm manufacturing rotary drills and employing 110. With Gainesville and the university so close, many Alachua residents commute to jobs there.

Spreading out in all directions from the Historic Main Street are pleasant residential sections with a mixture of old and new houses along streets lined with many giant live oak trees.

Several new housing developments have made their appearance in recent years, and, because of the expanded city limits, most are within the city. The most impressive of these developments has been Turkey Creek Golf and Racquet Club, six miles from the main part of town but still within Alachua. It's a wooded area with the houses built around an 18-hole golf course. About 300 families are living there in houses priced from around $50,000 to $400,000.

Just east of that development is Turkey Creek Forest, outside the city limits. The houses aren't as big and don't cost as much, but it's a very nice area, also heavily wooded. Prices for these houses range from $35,000 to $79,000 and are conventionally built. About 95 percent of the residents are retirees, mostly from the northeast and Midwest. There are 400 houses now, and there'll be 450 when the project is completed.

Those who favor outdoor recreational activities have a wide selection in the area northwest of Alachua. Ichetucknee Springs, noted for tubing in its 72 degrees temperature, is only 30 minutes away. O'Leno State Park is 10 miles away in the same direction, and Ginnie Springs, another of those spots with crystal clear water, is 12 miles away. Ginnie Springs may well be the most beautiful natural setting in Florida. It's unlikely there has been any change there since the Timucuan Indians and the Spanish explorers were circulating in the area. Most of the area around these parks and springs is wooded, and hunting for deer and small game is supposed to be good.

Fishermen find their best fresh water bet is the Santa Fe River, which is the northern border of Alachua County and about 10 miles from town. Those preferring salt water have only an hour's drive to the Gulf of Mexico and slightly more to the Atlantic.

In Alachua, the recreational needs of the community are well taken care of. A community center with a gym on the edge of town is surrounded by basketball, softball, football and tennis facilities, along with a Little League field and picnic grounds. Near the downtown area are two more tennis courts and another Little League field.

There's no hospital in Alachua, but there are three large hospitals in Gainesville with a total of over 1,000 beds and outstanding staffs. The town has a health clinic and also provides ambulance service to the hospitals.

A county library added to the scene in 1987 is open six days a week. The town's other cultural needs are largely satisfied by a wealth of offerings at the university, and some of the residents participate in its stage productions.

Santa Fe Community College is just 10 miles south of Alachua and offers a good selection of courses in adult education. Such classes also are available at the university.

A $1 million street paving project was started in 1988, and an electric substation will be built for $2.5 million. Also in the town's plans are apartment developments for low-income families and other low-cost housing that will replace dilapidated homes. Alachua has its own power, water and sewer systems. In something of a surprise move, the millage rate was lowered to $4.71 in 1988. The county's rate is about $21.

The town's biggest event each year is the Good Life Jubilee. Held in October, it draws over 10,000 people to an arts and crafts festival, miniature car races, a beauty pageant and live entertainment.

Out-of-state visitors should remember that this is north central Florida, not to be confused with the Florida keys. Temperatures dipped to a record low of seven degrees here during the killer freeze of 1985, so the bikinis are in storage during the winter months.

The annual growth rate is now about five percent, but this will undoubtedly increase. Even with the projected population increases, though, there is enough room to absorb that many people and still leave Alachua looking like a small town.

Belleview

Population 3,000. North Central. 10 miles south of Ocala. Development of 4,000 west of town. Community college in Ocala. Ocala National Forest nearby, good hunting and fishing. No large growth expected.

Though it's located in an area that's among the fastest growing in the U.S., Belleview has developed into one of the state's best small towns. A sleepy little settlement of retirees until the late 1970s, it has been able to handle the growth since then while retaining its small town flavor.

This north central Florida town had only 864 residents in 1960, and the many retirees there seemed quite content to relax and let the world slip by. Now Belleview has a population of 3,000 and is caught in a boom situation. It's part of the Ocala metropolitan area, and that area has grown by 48 percent in the 80s to a total population of 181,300. Only the Naples area in southwest Florida has surpassed it in the rate of growth.

There are 10 miles of largely rural areas separating Belleview from Ocala on the north, and that open space has allowed the place to preserve much of its small town flavor. But for the shopping centers on the edge of town, Belleview doesn't look much different than it did 40 years ago.

The retirees are still there, but now the percentage is down to about 30, as a younger crowd has been moving in to enjoy the quiet life-style. Many of these are people who commute to jobs in Ocala, then escape the traffic and congestion to return home and relax in Belleview.

In the areas surrounding Belleview on all sides the developers have been busy in recent years. The gently rolling countryside is now heavily populated, as the various subdivisions have been springing up within a short distance of town. Proof of this growth is a new post office, built in 1988 and serving 25,000 to 30,000 people. Largest of the developments has been Marion Oaks, just a few miles west of Belleview. There are 4,000 people there, and it's still growing.

East of Belleview, around Lake Weir, the largest lake in Marion County, it's a different world. This area has not undergone so drastic a change and is definitely rural. Here there are heavily wooded sections, the scenic Oklawaha River and many little lakes where the fish are biting and folks just lean back and ignore all that bustle a few miles away.

On the north side of Lake Weir and just about six miles from Belleview is the quiet, peaceful village of Oklawaha. Visitors have a tough time believing that the notorious Ma Barker and her son were gunned down by lawmen here back in the 1930s.

Only five miles north of Oklawaha is Moss Bluff, a favorite spot for boating and fishing on the Oklawaha River. The area around here has experienced little change over the years. It's right on the edge of the Ocala National Forest, a largely unspoiled wilderness that experiences a large invasion of hunters during the fall but is used mostly by campers and others just trying to get away from civilization for a few hours or days. It covers almost the entire eastern section of Marion County.

For a town that was so small for so long, Belleview has adapted well to the sudden influx of new residents. The town has been around for more than a century but didn't attract much attention until recent years.

Founded by John Pelot in 1884, Belleview was known in its early days as Long Swamp or Roach Pond. Since Belleview means beautiful view, that became the town's name, and incorporation followed in 1885, when there were 100 voters.

Advertised around the turn of the century as the health resort of Florida, Belleview attracted many settlers from New England. No alcohol was allowed within the city limits, and another local ordinance forbade hogs from roaming the streets, as they did in many Florida towns of that era. Benefitting from rail service to New York begun in the mid-1890s, the town drew many people who wanted to escape the northern winters, either for a visit or as a permanent home.

Long before the town was started, Seminole Indians roamed the area. In the late 1830s, these Indians and soldiers from the U.S. Army used to meet around a pond for night-long dances. The pond was then known as Nine Mile Pond, but it's now called Lake Lillian, and it's right in the middle of Belleview.

Amenities have been added as the town has grown and there is much to attract newcomers. There are quiet residential streets lined with large oaks, and some of the houses go back to the 19th century. A recreation park on the edge of town has two lighted ball fields, a soccer field, two lighted tennis courts and a playground for children. In the center of Belleview is Cherokee Park, an area designed for seniors. There are 16 lighted shuffleboard courts there and a building that's used for bingo, cards, suppers and meetings. A nine-hole golf course lies two miles from town and several 18-hole courses in Ocala and the surrounding area can be played. There is no swimming spot in Belleview, but Johnson's Beach on Lake Weir is only a few miles away and offers a sandy beach and a cool dip in clear waters.

The town has no hospital, but Munroe Regional Medical Center and Marion Community Hospital in Ocala each have over 300 beds and complete facilities.

In Belleview there's only one school, and that's at the elementary level. The older kids go to modern schools a few miles from town, but a new high school is planned for the near future. Adult education courses are available at Central Florida Community College in Ocala.

In town there's only one small industry, an apparel maker that employs about 60 people. Between Belleview and Ocala, though, there's a major employer, Certified Grocers. This is a wholesale grocery operation that employs nearly 1,000 people, many of them Belleview residents. The business covers eight acres, all under one roof.

Belleview residents apparently have been avid readers for a long time. The first library here was started in 1886, and the current library building was constructed in 1908. It houses 13,000 volumes and boasts the distinction of being the sixth oldest library in Florida. A little theater group is active and presents four productions each year in the auditorium in city hall, which was the town's school in earlier years.

Good housing is available in Belleview, and the prices are

45

reasonable. A home with three bedrooms and two baths will cost between $40,000 and $50,000. Those with one bath are usually priced below $45,000. The tax millage rate is $5.61.

The largest tourist attraction in the area is Silver Springs and its famous glass-bottomed boats east of Ocala.

All the growth of recent years astounds some of the older residents. One of them, Blanche Winters, when interviewed on her 90th birthday, observed that there had been more changes in the town in the last two years than in the 40 years before that. She came to Belleview as a little girl in 1900.

Still another old-timer, Frank Gale, was born in Belleview in 1898 in a house that was still standing when he turned 90. As a teenager, one of his first jobs was that of lamplighter, turning on the gas street lights. He tells of hunting alligators with a friend, capturing them alive and putting them in a pen to show northern visitors.

There are no alligator pens in Belleview now, but Lake Lillian is still around and is a favorite spot for children under 12 and seniors over 65. They are the only people allowed to fish there, and one youngster recently pulled out a panfish weighing two pounds.

Belleview is only one square mile in area, and unlikely to get any bigger. The residents are not opposed to annexing the outlying areas and increasing the town's tax base, but most living in those areas are not in favor of it.

For now, Belleview is satisfied with its status as a small town. It can tolerate the growth that has been occurring nearby and just hopes it can handle what lies ahead.

Crescent City

Population 1,900. North Central. 70 miles north of Orlando on U.S. 17. On large lake. Fern growing area. Many lakes nearby, good bass fishing. New library. Many retirees in winter. Annual Catfish Festival.

An automobile dealer who had spent 23 years in the urban sprawl of southeast Florida recently devoted two months to touring the state in search of a small town that had the quiet life-style he wanted. His search ended in Crescent City, a north central Florida town of only 1,900 population.

Located on U.S. Highway 17, about 30 miles north of DeLand and 20 miles south of Palatka, Crescent City is exactly the kind of place many new residents had in mind when they thought about a move to Florida. It's about as close to the typical small town as one's likely to find in this state. There's only one traffic light in town. Nobody's in a great rush, the kids are polite and the residents seem to care genuinely about each other.

For those looking for a town on a big lake good for fishing, this is the place to be. Crescent Lake, a scenic body of water 14 miles long and two miles wide, is on the east side of the town, and smaller Stella Lake is on the west side. Crescent Lake is used for fishing and boating, while a nice sandy beach on Lake Stella attracts the swimmers. On a ridge between the lakes, Crescent City goes about the business of savoring the slow-paced living that's been going on here for more than 100 years.

Incorporated in 1883, the town dates from as far back as 1852 when George Oliver got Crescent City started. Many families moved to the area after the Civil War. By 1870 a large citrus industry was prospering in and around Crescent City and continued to do so until 1894 when a devastating freeze wiped out nearly every citrus tree in Florida.

Undaunted by the citrus demise, the residents hit on the idea of raising ferns. Consequently, Crescent City has developed into one of the largest fern growing areas in the U.S., and the second largest in Florida.

Unconvinced by that 1894 freeze, some of the citrus growers replanted, and by the middle of this century thousands of acres of oranges and grapefruits were under cultivation. Then the Christmas freeze of 1983 hit, followed by another in early 1985. Again the citrus business became just a memory. This time the growers were apparently convinced, for fewer than 100 acres had been replanted five years later.

Meanwhile, the ferneries are continuing to prosper. Ferns have become Putnam County's number one crop with sales of $15.9 million in 1986—twice the value of the county's potato crop, the number two commodity. Only neighboring Volusia County produces more ferns than Putnam.

The area around Crescent City is blessed with all kinds of water. Dozens of small lakes lie just west of the town, and Lake George, Florida's second largest lake, is only eight miles away. Veteran fishermen will tell you that Lake George offers the best bass fishing anywhere in the U.S. Also offering good bass fishing as well as speckled perch and bream, Crescent Lake flows into Dunn's Creek, which in turn flows into the St. Johns River. The latter widens out north of Crescent City as it nears the completion of its course in Jacksonville.

Business in Crescent City is largely confined to Summit Street, which also is Highway 17. Only a couple blocks away is Crescent Lake where many impressive homes have been built. Some of the older frame homes, over 100 years old, stand right next to new concrete block homes. Prices of any homes along the lake are on the high side, usually over $100,000. Away from the lake prices drop to more reasonable figures. Good houses with three bedrooms are usually in the $50,000 range. The millage rate is $7.65 in the city and $14.58 in the county.

There's not much excitement around Crescent City, but that's the way most folks prefer it. Since the town's movie theater closed several years ago, much of the social activity now centers around the schools and churches. There's an elementary school in town, and the high school is four miles north on the highway.

"If you don't want to get bored to death, you better get involved in one or more of the various clubs in town," is the advice of a lady who's lived here since 1940.

About 60 percent of the population in the winter are retirees, though this figure drops to about 40 percent in the summer. There's no senior center in town, but the AARP has an active group that promotes bingo and other social events.

Aside from the ferneries in the area, the town's main source of employment is Miller Industries, started in 1922 by George C. Miller as a grocery store. Inheriting the business, his son, George C. Jr., has expanded it to include ten supermarkets and over 150 convenience stores throughout north and central

Florida. The firm's headquarters are in Crescent City, providing jobs for many of the town's residents. Other residents commute to jobs with the Georgia Pacific Co. paper mills in Palatka, and some even drive to work in DeLand and Daytona Beach, 45 minutes away.

The town is without a hospital, but the Crescent City Public Health Center opened in 1956 under the sponsorship of the Business and Professional Women's Club. The city provides ambulance service to hospitals in Palatka, DeLand and Daytona Beach.

A recent addition to the local scene is the public library. Housing 11,000 volumes, it is in an attractive brick building that opened in 1987 after the town raised $87,000 to match a similar grant from the state. Nearby, along the highway, the Women's Club, organized in 1890, has another impressive building.

The high school has the usual athletic facilities, while in town there are tennis courts in one of the city parks and a Little League facility built with $30,000 raised from selling catfish dinners.

How can you raise $30,000 from catfish dinners? You do it by having a Catfish Festival, and Crescent City has been doing it since the late 70s. The event is held the first Saturday in April in a park along the highway. The most recent one attracted 30,000 people, each paying $5 for a large plate of fried fingerling catfish, cole slaw and hush puppies. For those still hungry after that, separate servings of swamp cabbage, alligator tails, steamed blue crab and catfish chowder are available for small fees. Those 30,000 people last year ate 7,000 pounds of catfish.

The festival is a day-long event that also includes a parade, an arts and crafts show, a catfish skinning contest, blue grass music, a five kilometer run and bicycle rides of distances up to 100 miles. Money from the festival, and there's lots of it with 30,000 people paying $5 each, has been used for worthwhile projects like the Little League field. Over $100,000 has provided scholarships for local high school graduates who couldn't afford college. Every needy graduate in the last five years received from $800 to $2000.

Single mobile homes are not allowed in Crescent City, but a park for recreation vehicles is operating after winning a lawsuit when the town banned them.

Aside from that lawsuit, there has been little in recent years to disturb the tranquility around Crescent City. Old-timers still remember the fight over Highway 17 going through the town in the 1920s. Most opposed it, but the highway still was built. Earlier, another generation had rejected the railroad's attempt to send trains through Crescent City on a route from Jacksonville to Key West. They thought the steamboats on the rivers were all the transportation they needed, little realizing the railroads would eventually put the steamboats out of business.

It's not that Crescent City is fighting progress. It's just that the citizens like their little town the way it is and are not interested in any major changes.

McIntosh

Population 415. North Central. 17 miles north of Ocala on U.S. 441. Good scenery, quiet. Hilly town, many Victorian houses. Large horse farms in area. 1890s Festival each fall. On Orange Lake, good fishing. Some retirees.

For those seeking the quiet life, good scenery and a small town with a rich history, McIntosh, the most comprehensive Victorian town in Florida, is the ideal location.

Only 415 people live here, but there are many more trees than that and a hilly landscape in this Marion County town situated about halfway between Ocala and Gainesville on U.S. Highway 441.

Some of the residents are retirees, but much of the population is made up of young couples who came here to raise a family. Though lacking some of the amenities, McIntosh is one of Florida's prettiest small towns. Those making their first visit here are always impressed with the physical beauty, and the quiet is overwhelming.

"The trees make the town," is the observation of one of McIntosh's oldest citizens. And there can be no quarrel with that. Giant live oaks, most planted at the turn of the century, line the streets, their long strands of Spanish moss hanging almost to the ground in many places. Those trees and the many Victorian houses in town are the first items to catch one's attention upon entering McIntosh.

A rural Victorian community on the old Florida Southern Railroad, much of the town is designated as a historic district including most of the residential and business areas of the original plat of 1885.

Despite its small size, McIntosh has experienced a lengthy and exciting history. Little was recorded about it before 1882, though botanist William Bartram described groves of wild oranges in an area near the Seminole settlement of Cuscowilla, about eight miles north of where McIntosh is now, when he explored the Florida peninsula in the 1780s. Cuscowilla later became Micanopy, the state's oldest inland town.

From the 1870s until the big freeze in 1895, oranges were the major crop around McIntosh, having replaced sugar and cotton as the leading moneymakers. Grafted into the wild stock already established in the region, the fruit was shipped to a ferry on nearby Orange Lake, from there to Palatka, then north by way of the St. Johns River.

When the oranges were wiped out by the freeze in '95, area farmers turned to vegetables, which dominated the scene until the Everglades were drained in the late 20s and early 30s. Before that happened and the vegetable industry moved to south Florida, many fortunes were made by truck farmers around McIntosh. One farmer grew nothing but iceberg lettuce for the liner *Queen Mary*, shipping it by box cars to New York.

Much of the land devoted to vegetables over a half century ago is now the site for the magnificent horse farms that dot the countryside around here. Marion County has become one of the country's prime areas for thoroughbred breeding, and its hills are covered with green pastures, white wooden fences and some of the priciest horse flesh in captivity.

A few farmers who saw the vegetable empire dissolve in

McIntosh returned to citrus, and about 1,500 acres of oranges were planted in the immediate area. Then another killer freeze struck on Christmas morning of 1983, and citrus in Marion County was probably doomed forever. Only about 20 acres have been replanted since, and even that investment is a large gamble.

Now most of the McIntosh citizens commute to jobs in Ocala, 17 miles away, or Gainesville, 15 miles away. Many driving to Gainesville are connected with the University of Florida.

Long-time residents of McIntosh are proud of the town's past and have made tremendous efforts to preserve it, including the successful battle to save the town depot. Built around 1895 and threatened with extinction when the last train passed through McIntosh in 1974, the depot had been the center of activity in the days when vegetable farming was still big and the tourists were arriving by train to fish in Orange Lake or hunt in the nearby area. It would take considerable money to save that depot, move it 26 feet and preserve some of the railroad track.

How to accomplish this with no funds on hand? The town's old-timers got together and hit on the idea of having an 1890s Festival. They called themselves Friends of McIntosh, and that first festival in 1974 drew 3,500 people, not bad for a start. By the next year it was 6,000. In 1988, the number had swelled to 40,000, which is about 100 times the population of the town. Imagine trying to find parking space for 40,000 people in a town of 400! They manage to do it by scheduling the event on a weekend when the University of Florida football team is not playing in Gainesville. Held in October or November, the festival includes a tour of the Victorian homes, a parade, barbecue, about 300 arts and crafts booths and a bagpipe band that lends the event a Scottish flavor.

The depot, naturally, was saved and renovated and is now getting readied as the town's museum.

Four-laned highway 441 bisects the town. Businesses are on both sides, but most of the older houses are on the east. With so small a population and two large cities so near, the businesses are limited to a grocery, a drug store, a hardware, a garage and a couple of offices for real estate firms.

Down at the bottom of the hill from the highway and not far from Orange Lake sits the town's brick post office. Just outside is the community bulletin board, on which folks rely for news of what's happening in town.

"Water will be off Monday Dec. 5 for about two hours, beginning at 8:00 A.M.," reads a handwritten note on letterhead stationery from the Town of McIntosh. Another notice reads, "WANTED, new home for world's greatest cats, going overseas in December." With the notice are pictures of the cats. Other notes tell about missing or found pets and garage sales. For those who grew up in small towns, all of this will sound familiar.

There is no school here. There had been 70 children in grades kindergarten through 12 back in the early part of this century. Later the town lost the high school, and the elementary school was closed about 25 years ago. Now the kids are bused to schools elsewhere in the county.

A bookmobile from a library in the nearby town of Reddick serves the town's reading needs. There are large hospitals in both Ocala and Gainesville. The town has a dentist and doctor, a volunteer fire department and a sheriff's office that handles police duties.

About 75 years ago McIntosh had a hotel, which is now a home. A weekly newspaper operated until the 1940s. The printing presses and trays of hand-set type remain as they were used on the final edition of the paper.

The town council meets in a civic center in Van Ness Park, where a tennis court and playground equipment for small children are also located.

Despite so few residents, the four churches in town appear prosperous. The oldest is the Methodist, built in 1890 and moved by a lone mule pulling it over logs from a little settlement a mile and a half away to its present location. The other churches are Christian, Baptist and Presbyterian, all built in the distant past.

The town's only industry is a small company that makes duct work for air conditioning. There are no attempts to attract more. Housing costs are reasonable. Three-bedroom, two-bath homes about three years old sell for approximately $90,000. Larger houses run from $110,000 to $200,000, while an acre and a quarter of land costs about $15,000. McIntosh's tax millage rate is $2.90.

Though those wanting a game of golf have to travel to Ocala or Gainesville, fishing enthusiasts have just a short walk to Orange Lake and some of the best fishing in Florida. Here 16,000 acres offer prime fishing for bass and various pan fish. Hunting is also good in the area.

In a town so small it's remarkable there are over 30 homes dating back to the 19th century. That so many of them survived is largely due to folks not having enough money to build newer homes after the produce business foundered. Now these homes, built of hard yellow pine, and described architecturally as Victorian Gothic, in two stories, are among the town's greatest assets.

How McIntosh got its name is still something of a mystery. One of the favorite theories deals with a George Houstoun who wrote in his diary in 1851 about Col. John Houstoun McIntosh, owner of a plantation in the 1820s that may have included the land where the town is now. The plantation was later ruined and his sugar mill burned by Indians during the second Seminole War of 1835–42. Although McIntosh took off, he played a major role in the early history around here, and may have been the source of the town's name.

Now McIntosh has become largely a bedroom community for Ocala and Gainesville. Aside from the 1890s Festival, the only event in town is an annual Quilt Festival in the spring, also sponsored by the Friends of McIntosh. Those attending that event are further entertained by the sight of all the azaleas and dogwood trees in bloom then. With the new growth on the oak trees, the town is a real wonderland of nature.

Folks who live in McIntosh tell you they like the slow pace of living and how easy it is to get acquainted with everyone. That anything around this town would ever change is most unlikely. It wouldn't be McIntosh if it did.

Micanopy

Population 737. North Central. 11 miles south of Gainesville. Oldest inland town in state. Many antique shops. Rich, colorful history. Paynes Prairie, wilderness area, nearby. Very quiet, many trees.

OSCEOLA

MICANOPY, FLORIDA

A Timucua Indian village of the Potano tribe was located near here when the early Spanish explorer Hernando De Soto led his expedition through the area in 1539. Botanist William Bartram visited Cuscawilla village nearby in 1774. The first permanent white settlement in what is now Alachua County, called Wanton, was started in 1821. Wanton Post Office was established in 1826, the name was changed to Micanopy in 1834. Fort Micanopy, also called Fort Defiance, stood near here during the Second Seminole War. Several skirmishes were fought nearby. The town was incorporated September 15, 1858.

As long as 7,000 years ago, Indians occupied the present site of Micanopy, Florida's oldest inland town.

While Florida has been experiencing explosive population growth through the last four decades, there are a few locations where time has virtually stood still. No better example of this is Micanopy, the oldest inland town in the state. When Micanopy was incorporated in 1880, 59 years after it was established in 1821, the head count was about 600. More than a century later the total has reached only 737.

The town was platted way back in the early part of the 19th century as one square mile. In all the years since the size has not changed. Located on the southern edge of Alachua County, 11 miles from Gainesville and the University of Florida, Micanopy is a town of trees, hundreds of them in that one square mile. Giant oak trees well over a century old, magnolias, dogwoods and a variety of others keep most of the village in the summer in perpetual shade. Many of the houses were built in the 19th century. It's always quiet here, real quiet.

Once a bustling business center, Micanopy is now a town devoted almost exclusively to antiques. The main street, which used to be U.S. Highway 441 before that road was routed just outside the town, has more than a dozen antique shops. With no other businesses around, folks need a car to drive into Gainesville, a city of over 75,000, to buy their groceries. They don't seem to mind, since living costs in Micanopy are far less than in most Florida communities.

While Gainesville is such a short distance away, Micanopy residents don't worry about the city expanding and swallowing them up a few years from now. Paynes Prairie a mile away has taken care of that for all time.

A wilderness of 18,000 acres, Paynes Prairie has been a state preserve since 1970. Although bisected by Interstate 75 and 441, it's an area full of wildlife. In the town's earliest days, this area was a lake used for shipping produce by barge to the railroad. The lake filled and emptied from time to time, depending on the flow of water in underground passages. In 1892 it suddenly went dry and has been a prairie ever since.

Few towns in the state have a more interesting history than Micanopy, despite its small size. The Timucuan Indians were early settlers in the region and were found by Spanish explorer Hernando de Soto on his expedition through the area in the

16th century. Indeed, excavations have revealed that Indians were here as long ago as 7,000 years.

In 1774, William Bartram, the great Quaker naturalist of Philadelphia, made a trip through the southeast, collecting botanical specimens. He visited the Seminole chief, Cowkeeper, at the Indian village of Cuscowilla, now Micanopy. His accounts of the flora and fauna and vivid images of local scenes were an inspiration for writers Coleridge, Wordsworth and Emerson.

The first white settlement in what is now Alachua County was called Wanton and was founded in 1821. A post office was established there in 1826. In 1834 the name was changed to Micanopy after an Indian chief who was the nominal head of the Seminole Nation in 1821, when Florida became the property of the U.S. and ceased being Spanish territory.

Troubles with the Indians persisted from the founding through much of the next two decades, and Fort Micanopy was built in 1837 to fend off the Seminoles. Several skirmishes were fought nearby, but the white men finally prevailed and Micanopy became a thriving community.

A man named Moses Levy had a plantation there in 1823. Spending considerable money to develop the area, he brought sugar cane from Havana and built a sugar mill and storage houses. In half a century, there were vast orange groves in the area, and schools, churches, hotels, stores, a grist mill and a cotton mill. A total of 100,000 boxes of oranges were shipped from Micanopy annually. Soon a mutual fire insurance company had executive offices in the town, and a local newspaper had been established. The leading industry was the production of great quantities of fruits and vegetables for the northern market. In the winter of 1894–95, twin freezes struck Micanopy. The temperature dipped to 11 degrees and snow fell. The young trees were killed to the ground and the old trees so damaged they died. Fortunes were swept away in a single night.

These folks were a hardy lot, though, and they bounced back to replant the orange groves. By 1903 the first carload of oranges was shipped from Micanopy, and in 1915 there were orange trees on all sides of the town. As recently as the late 1920s there was a basket factory, sawmills, a turpentine plant, two hotels, several stores, cafes and a high school in town.

The Great Depression followed, several more freezes hit, the roads were rerouted around Micanopy, and the town became the sleepy little place it is now. Those who live here love it, and for good reason. Even at high noon it's quiet enough to hear the birds sing and the squirrels scamper up and down the big oak trees. Everyone knows everyone else in town, and they're all friendly. A University of Florida professor bought an old Victorian house here eight years ago, after a long tour of duty at Northwestern University near Chicago. He and his wife were so smitten with Micanopy, they bought a plot in the village cemetery and thereby announced to their fellow residents they were here to stay.

That cemetery, almost as old as Micanopy, is a beautiful little spot on the edge of town with lots of those massive oak trees. Interred there is a James W. Martin, born in 1737 and died in 1826, and believed to be the first person buried here.

Despite all the quiet, the citizens aren't exactly napping. Much of the town's activities center around the three churches, Baptist, Methodist and Episcopalian. The Episcopal church dates from 1870 and is still a meeting place for local groups. There are several artists in town, including weavers and potters, and an arts and crafts fall festival is held every year. With the university so close, those who like the many concerts, art shows and other entertainment offered there throughout the year don't have far to travel.

Fishermen and hunters can also find nearby facilities. Orange Lake, one of the state's prime fishing areas, is only two miles south and east of Micanopy, and the Lochloosa Wildlife Management Area is just east of town.

There's no hospital here, but excellent facilities are available in three large hospitals in Gainesville. A public health nurse and paramedics are among the full-time employees at the town's fire station. The sheriff's office handles what few police duties there are.

For the seniors, and there are quite a few, the town offers a Meals on Wheels program with a van delivering meals and helping on errands, including doctors appointments.

Micanopy is without a school, so all the kids are bused to Gainesville. There was a school in town, but the integration hassle of the 1960s brought an end to that. Now the school has become the town hall and library. The latter is open four days a week.

The town has a recreation center, a sports area near the fire station, including an outdoor basketball court, and a Little League field. The closest thing to a hotel is the Herlong Mansion. Built in 1821, it has been remodeled several times since and is now a bed and breakfast spot. A museum is being planned by the Micanopy Historical Society and will occupy space in a warehouse opposite the fire station.

With so little space left in a town that's been around so long, there isn't much building going on. Even so, there are a few lots still available, and there have been 14 housing starts in the last three years. The town's millage rate is $6.34.

For the tourists, aside from the plethora of antique shops, there's Cross Creek and Paynes Prairie. Cross Creek is the little place nine miles from Micanopy where Marjorie Kinnan Rawlings wrote *The Yearling* and other lasting novels. Her rustic home is open to visitors daily except Tuesday and Wednesday.

Paynes Prairie is among the most significant natural and historic areas of the state and was the center of man's activities in Florida for many centuries. Many Indian artifacts have been found there, as well as evidence of a Spanish cattle ranch in the 1600s.

There are all kinds of waterfowl in this large preserve, 20 wild horses and six bisons, in addition to many deer and small game. Both tourists and area residents enjoy boating, fishing, picnicking and swimming at Lake Wauberg within the preserve.

An attractive visitor center offering many exhibits on the natural and cultural history of the preserve is worth a visit, as is an observation tower near the center with a good view.

One of Micanopy's most famous residents was Archie Carr, the world's leading authority on sea turtles. He lived in Micanopy for 37 years and did most of his writing here before he died in 1987. Most of the residents commute to jobs in Ocala and Gainesville, but they are always happy to get home at the end of each day and savor a square mile of the state that has escaped the inroads of "progress." Very little ever changes in Micanopy, and that's what makes it delightful.

Trenton

Population 1,200. North Central. 28 miles west of Gainesville. Watermelons, dairying main agricultural interests. Many residents commute to jobs in Gainesville. Some retirees. Eight miles from Suwannee River, good fishing.

When a man from one of Florida's largest cities was planning to visit a real estate agent in the town of Trenton recently, he asked for directions and was told, "I'm just one block west of the only traffic light in Gilchrist County."

In a state that has grown as fast as Florida, it's hard to imagine a county with only a single traffic light. But in this north central part of the state growth has come slowly, and Gilchrist is just one of several counties with populations in four figures.

Gilchrist and its county seat of Trenton came close to being absorbed by another county less than ten years ago. The census of 1960 showed only 2,868 people living in the county and fewer than 1,000 in Trenton. This had been a decrease from the 1950 head count, and folks realized it would be increasingly difficult to keep a county solvent with so few taxpayers. They actually explored the possibility of consolidating with another county. The final decision was to keep trying it alone, and by the 1970 census nearly 700 new residents had been added to the roll. The population reached almost 6,000 by 1980, and now it's close to 10,000. The county's bad days are behind it, and the people around Trenton are definitely optimistic.

The population of Trenton now is about 1,200, but it's the

largest town in the county and one of only three incorporated. Bell and Fanning Springs, the other two, are much smaller.

It's been over a century since a man named Ben Boyd established a sawmill in the town of Joppa. Boyd had been a native of Trenton, Tenn., and decided to have the name of Joppa changed to Trenton.

There was no Gilchrist County until 1925, when it became the last Florida county formed. Prior to that it had been part of Alachua County, but a dispute arose over the need for a new road from the Suwannee River at the western edge of the county to Gainesville, home of the state university. Folks around Trenton demanded the road and threatened to withdraw from Alachua if it wasn't built. The county officials called their bluff and told them to go ahead and form their own county, which they proceeded to do.

In the years since, the county has been largely agricultural. The major crop is watermelons, while peanuts, pecans, corn, sorghum and hay also are grown in large quantities. Four dairy farms near Trenton employ about 250 people.

Only in current years has the economy experienced the

Only eight miles from Trenton, the Suwannee River offers excellent boating, fishing and swimming.

invasion of new industries. A few miles from Trenton a minimum security prison was built by the state in the early 80s, and this provides employment for about 200. A boat manufacturer and a furniture maker employ about 80 more, and 1988 brought the announcement of a much larger employer: the Ginnie Springs Bottling Co., a firm which will have more than 100 employees. The company will bottle two million gallons of crystal clear water daily from Ginnie Springs in the northern part of the county. This $15 million operation will have its own truck terminal, manufacture its own bottles and distribute the water by trucks all over the U.S.

For Trenton and the rest of the county a firm of that size is welcome news. Up to now 73 percent of the non-agricultural work force in the county has been working in Alachua County. The city of Gainesville lies about 28 miles to the east of Trenton, and many are employed there.

Pleasant little Trenton keeps itself tidy and has more amenities than most places of such modest size. Most businesses are confined to a single street with good residential sections along shaded streets behind the business district.

The courthouse, recently expanded, sits at the corner of that lone traffic light, and the high school is at the other end of Main Street.

For new residents, as well as those already here, one of the greatest inducements for living in Trenton is the absence of any real estate taxes. The town can function with the income from the state gas tax and sales tax. In the county the tax millage rate is $16.95.

Until recent years, the area had attracted few retirees, but they have been discovering Trenton and the rest of Gilchrist County. Quite a few young people have also been migrating here.

At a time when crime dominates the news in most towns and cities, it's refreshing to find a place where people tell you they don't have to lock their doors at night. Some even park their cars on Main Street and leave their keys in the ignition.

Recreation is important in Trenton, and the residents don't have far to go to find it. The historic Suwannee River, only eight miles west of Trenton, offers excellent fishing, swimming and boating. There are six springs in the area, and the most popular one is about ten miles from Trenton. That's Hart Springs, a county-maintained park used for swimming, camping and picnics and offering dozens of covered picnic tables in a pretty setting. The nearest golf facility is an 18-hole course in Chiefland, 11 miles away.

Trenton's neat little park near the town's community building has two tennis courts, racquetball courts and a softball field. The community building is used for a Meals on Wheels program by the AARP, the 4-H Club and for family reunions and other functions.

There's no hospital yet in Trenton, but one with 50 beds will be built soon six miles from town. Meanwhile, Trenton has the J. Min Ayers Medicare Nursing Center. The facility has 120 beds and was built in the early 80s after the town's newspaper publisher donated the land for it. He's the J. Min Ayers the building was named for, and he's been with the paper since 1934, when he went to work as a reporter for $8 a week.

Despite its small size, Trenton also has a library, open five days a week. It's the Suwannee River Regional Library for Gilchrist County and has about 10,000 books.

North of Trenton consideration is being given to the purchase by the state of 45,000 acres for a state forest. It would be used for hunting, fishing and camping.

Back in the early days of this county the area was one vast forest of pines, hardwoods and cedar. The early settlers cleared the trees, and all large timber was eliminated. It is on this cleared land that all the various crops are now being raised.

Real estate prices in Trenton and the nearby areas are reasonable. Houses with three bedrooms and one and a half baths may be purchased for $35,000. Most home construction, though, is outside Trenton because of limited space in town. Mobile homes are banned in some areas of Trenton but are allowed near the nursing center.

The stores in Trenton are adequate, and shoppers needing big items have plenty of selection in Gainesville.

With the climb toward the 10,000 mark in population, local

observers have noted a steady influx of people from other Florida cities, particularly the Tampa–St. Petersburg and Miami areas. One man, employed in Miami by the Treasury Department for many years and planning to retire soon, made a cross-state bicycle trip a few years ago and liked what he saw in Trenton. When retirement arrived, he drove to Trenton, bought a house and is still here.

An excellent school system in the county has been a major selling point in attracting new residents. For those interested in adult education courses, the university and a community college in Gainesville offer a wide range of subjects.

The people of Trenton and surrounding Gilchrist County feel they are on the brink of experiencing some of the same growth that has been happening in most other areas of Florida. The annual growth rate in recent years has been 20 to 25 percent, and projections call for the county population to double in the next five years. Much of that growth is expected in the little village of Bell, north of Trenton, while still more will occur from the Alachua County line westward.

For a county that almost ceased to exist such a short time ago, Gilchrist has made a remarkable recovery. And the folks around Trenton are elated over the better days that have arrived for their little town.

4. NORTHEAST

Fernandina Beach

Population 8,500. Northeast. 35 miles north of Jacksonville. On island in Atlantic, near Georgia. Downtown area restored to turn-of-century look. Colorful history. Two large paper mills. Shrimp Festival annually.

One of the best kept secrets in Florida has to be Fernandina Beach. Tucked away in the extreme northeast corner of the state, this town has much to offer both visitors and residents. Tourists bypass it and few Floridians know anything about it, but Fernandina Beach is well worth a look.

Fernandina Beach is on Amelia Island with the Atlantic Ocean on one side and the Intracoastal Waterway on the other. Only the St. Marys River separates the city from Georgia. It's the county seat of Nassau County, about 35 miles north of Jacksonville.

Few towns in Florida have a longer or more colorful history than Fernandina Beach. It's been here since the 17th century and is the only place in the U.S. to have existed under eight different flags. A recent, major development in the city's history, and one that placed it high on the list of Florida's best attractions, occurred in the 1970s when a 30-block area of the downtown was restored to its appearance at the turn of the century. Touring it now is like a trip in a time capsule to the Victorian era.

Prior to this undertaking, Fernandina Beach had experienced a remarkable history as the French, Spanish and British took turns in controlling the island. Not until 1821, when

Spain ceded Florida to the U.S., did Fernandina Beach come out from under foreign rule.

The island was first invaded in 1562 by Jean Ribault, a French explorer. Just three years later the Spanish took over, established a post there in 1686 and kept control until 1763. Meanwhile, General James Oglethorpe, founder of Georgia, established a post and named the island in honor of Princess Amelia, sister of King George II, in 1735. The Spanish and British then played something of a tug of war with the island until President Monroe's action in 1821.

By the 1850s Fernandina was forced to move from what was called Old Town in a marshy area to higher ground that would permit the building of a railroad. Florida's first senator, David Levy Yulee, built this 155-mile railroad from Fernandina to Cedar Key, the state's first cross-state railroad.

By 1875 Fernandina was entering its greatest era of prosperity, when tourists were flocking to the town via steamers from New York to stay in two elegant hotels. This era lasted until around 1900, when Henry Flagler built his railroad

Centre Street, Fernandina Beach, restored to its original Victorian appearance.

The elegant Palace Saloon, one of Florida's oldest, serves customers from a hand-carved mahogany bar.

through peninsula Florida and bypassed Fernandina. The tourists then followed the railroad, and Fernandina entered a long period of decline. Fortunately, the buildings in the business district, despite the hard times, weren't torn down and were available when the residents seized on the idea of restoring them to their elegance of a century ago.

Now Fernandina Beach has something unmatched elsewhere in Florida. No other town has done such an extensive restoration of its commercial district. The old buildings, along three blocks of Centre Street, house fashionable shops, good restaurants, the usual run of retail stores and the Empire Saloon, Florida's oldest saloon in the original location. The latter has been there since 1903 and features a handcarved mahogany bar, large mirror, pressed tin ceiling and murals painted in 1907. At the end of the restored area is the county courthouse, built in 1891 and still in use. On the side streets off Centre Street are many fine old mansions, their architectural gingerbread beautifully restored.

On top of all this history and rich heritage, Fernandina

Beach has become a very modern and vibrant city. It has a sound economy and boasts a good life-style with heavy emphasis on the arts and water sports. The population is about 8,500, and the small town environment has been well preserved. Two paper mills, Container Corporation of America and ITT Rayonier, have 1,350 employees and are the two largest industries. Unemployment is only 4.8 percent. Fishing still is a major source of income here. The modern shrimping industry was founded in Fernandina Beach early in this century, and many boats still ply their trade from here. Several boats may be chartered for either fishing or sightseeing.

All this activity originates from Fernandina Harbour Marina, which was renovated in 1986. The marina has an 800-foot floating breakwater and 94 floating concrete slips that can handle sailboats, power boats, fishing and sailing charters, yachts and even the great cruise ships that stop for a few hours or overnight.

Just a short distance from Fernandina Beach is the Amelia Island Plantation, a privately owned resort and residential community that was carved out of a wilderness next to the ocean and has been operating since 1974. There are 1,200 units there and 300 permanent families in residence. Prices range from $78,000 for a condo with two bedrooms and an ocean view to single family homes close to $250,000. The development is one of the area's leading employers with 900 people on the payroll.

Golf and tennis play a major role at the Plantation. There are 45 holes for the golfers and 25 tennis courts. Two big tennis tournaments are held there each year. The All American Championships for men and women is staged in September, and an official stop on the women's professional circuit is held in April, offering nearly $300,000 in prizes.

This development, as well as the rest of Amelia Island, is likely to be annexed by Fernandina Beach, and that will double the current population. The island is 13.5 miles long and one-fourth mile to two miles wide.

Tourism is a big business in town. Although Fernandina Beach is ignored by most Floridians, residents from nearby

Georgia and South Carolina pour in here during the summer to enjoy a wonderful four-mile long beach on the Atlantic.

As a kickoff to the summer season, the city holds its largest event of the year, the Shrimp Festival, on the first weekend in May. It's been held since the 1960s and draws crowds of well over 100,000, mostly from Georgia and Jacksonville. There are 70 arts and crafts booths, many food booths and 35 antique booths, plus live entertainment.

Recreational activities and the arts receive heavy attention throughout the year. In addition to the facilities for boating and fishing from the renovated marina and the excellent beach and nearby park, there are two swimming pools, four lighted tennis courts, two public golf courses and two softball fields.

The Amelia Community Theater puts on four productions each year at Fernandina High School. The local Arts Alliance is composed of 60 performing artists. There's also an Amelia Island choral music group that stages four productions annually. In October, Fernandina Beach spotlights the arts with a sidewalk arts and crafts show that extends over three weekends in the downtown area.

On a side street in the downtown area is a library that was built in the late 1970s and has 28,000 volumes. Since it's a branch of the Jacksonville library system, local residents have access to all the books in the Jacksonville library by just requesting them.

Somewhat isolated as it is, Fernandina Beach is fortunate to have its own hospital, Nassau General, with 54 beds and full services. It serves all of Nassau County.

The nearest college is Florida Community College in Jacksonville, but adult education courses are held in the local middle school on a year-round basis.

Though living costs are about 10 percent higher than in most of north Florida, good homes are still available for under $50,000. Single mobile homes are not allowed in the city, but there is one mobile home park in the city and two in the county. The millage rate is $8 in town, $16 in the county.

Unlike Florida cities farther south, there is no large concentration of senior retirees here, though there are quite a few young retirees in the city and at Amelia Island Plantation. The percentage of folks over 65 is 21.1, and a senior center operates five days a week.

Visitors to Fernandina Beach are attracted by more than just the restored area and the beach. Fort Clinch State Park, several blocks from downtown, offers camping, fishing, swimming and boating. The park was a fort when the Civil War started and was occupied by Confederate forces until retaken by federal troops, who also occupied the town of Fernandina during the balance of the war.

Also near downtown the Amelia Island Museum, open Monday through Saturday, provides an interesting look at the area's history.

It's really hard to believe that so many Florida residents and those outside the state don't know about Fernandina Beach. This is a town with enough history to fill several volumes and a future that holds great promise.

5. CENTRAL

Auburndale

Population 8,000. Central. 25 miles south of Disney World. In citrus belt. 26 diversified industries. Outstanding recreational facilities. Hospital. Senior center. 14 lakes in town. Two colleges nearby.

For those shopping for a small town to settle in, Auburndale may be the answer. At least the town's slogan, "The Hometown People Are Looking For," says this is the place.

Auburndale is another of those Florida towns that barely escaped disaster when the killing freezes of 1983 and 1985 struck the state's citrus belt. U. S. Highway 92 running through the middle of the town, east to west, was something of a dividing line when the record cold hit. Many of the groves north of the highway were wiped out, while only a few south of it suffered significant damage.

Citrus still is a major industry around here, but there is much more economic diversification now than before the twin freezes. Other new industries unrelated to citrus have moved in and provided a badly needed shot in the arm for the local economy. Still, Auburndale is in Polk County, the biggest citrus producing county in the U. S., and many residents just step into the backyard and pull oranges and grapefruit off the trees for breakfast each morning.

The population passed the 8,000 mark late in 1988, but the small town spirit still dominates. If all the big city amenities aren't here, they're only a short drive away. It's just four miles to Winter Haven, a city of 25,000, and nine miles to Lakeland, a city of 50,000. Walt Disney World is only 25 miles up the road, and Tampa is 50 miles to the west.

A quick trip around town tells you this is a town with a fierce interest in recreational facilities. Most conversations with the residents aren't long before these facilities are mentioned. They are a considerable source of pride, and justly so.

In the downtown area, just a short walk from city hall, are eight tennis courts and a pro shop, 18 shuffleboard courts, eight basketball goals and two full-sized courts—all lighted. Across the street a building houses eight lighted four-wall racquetball courts with pro shop and showers.

Scattered around the rest of the town are two lighted Little League fields with concession stands and press box, a lighted Senior League baseball field, a girls softball field with clubhouse, concession stand and conference room, two lighted softball fields for men and women, three junior high softball fields, five softball fields for the high school, a lighted soccer and band practice field, senior horseshoe pits, two men's softball fields, basketball courts and volleyball courts at another recreation center, three softball fields and five youth soccer fields at the elementary school and a lighted baseball field for a town team—all of this in a town that just reached 8,000 population.

Auburndale residents are proud of their sports facilities, a short walk from city hall, above.

Auburndale doesn't have a golf course, but there are good 18-hole courses in nearby Winter Haven and Lakeland and one of the finest courses in the state about ten miles away in Haines City.

For those leaning toward water sports, an outstanding public beach is on Lake Ariana, the town's largest lake and the one around which the town has developed over the years. Pollution, which has ruined so many of Florida's lakes, hasn't affected Lake Ariana. The large sandy beach has a roped-off area for swimmers, a fishing pier and a boat ramp for easy access into the water. Along the beach are many covered picnic tables, grills and lots of playground equipment. In a separate building the Ariana Beach Yacht Club stays active on a year-round basis. Fourteen smaller lakes are located throughout town, though several would be better described as ponds.

Across from the tennis and shuffleboard courts downtown, is an attractive complex that includes a civic center, a library and a senior center, which is the latest addition built in 1981. The library, now housing 34,000 volumes, is open daily except Sunday and needs to be expanded. The senior center offers arts and crafts classes, congregate meals, Meals on Wheels and exercise classes. A Tourist Club also operates in this building and has 250 members who pay individual dues of $9 per year. The civic center is used for all types of functions, including meetings of many clubs, musical programs and other entertainment.

Since 1976, the one special event held in Auburndale annually is a blue-grass festival, one of the largest in the country, which takes place on three days in March. Blue-grass fans come from all over the U.S. to hear musicians compete for prizes. Held in a city park downtown and sponsored with the help of local business, the event is free. Just donations are requested.

Though the town attracts many retirees, there is no accurate account of how many. Most are from the northeast and Michigan. One retiree, who has been in Auburndale for several years, tells of making a well organized tour of the state's small towns and cities before settling on Auburndale because it had so many amenities and the lowest cost of living of all those checked.

While there are excellent hospitals in Lakeland, Auburndale still has its own, Murrow Memorial, a facility with 38 beds. It doesn't have emergency facilities but offers cosmetic surgery.

In addition to the wealth of recreation facilities, the citizens take great pride in their education system. In an era when so many elementary and high schools are beset with disciplinary problems, Auburndale has maintained the older values and enforces law and order in its system. The town also has a school that offers arts and crafts courses for dropouts and a wide range of subjects for adults. Polk Community College in Winter Haven also provides a varied curriculum for adults, and Florida Southern College, a well-regarded four-year institution, is in Lakeland.

With 26 industries in town, there's very little worry about unemployment. The largest industry is Coca-Cola, which specializes in citrus concentrate and employs 600 to 650 workers. Next largest is Fleetwood Homes, a manufacturer of mobile homes that employs another 400 to 500. Other major employers are Adams Packing, citrus concentrate, 280 employees; Colorado Boxed Beef Co., food distributor, 175 employees; Dial Corp., bottles and bleach, 135 employees; Fuque Homes, mobile homes, 150 employees; International Paper Co., corrugated shipping containers, 150 employees; Owens Corning Fiberglass, underground storage tanks, 100 employees, and Sedco Pipe Products, plastic pipes, 150 employees. Scotty's, one of the largest lumber suppliers in the southeast, has its corporate offices in Auburndale.

There are four industrial parks in the town and plenty of room for expansion. With all this industry and the town's steady growth in recent years, it's difficult to realize this area was mostly wilderness just a century ago.

A man named William Van Fleet was largely responsible for starting much of the development that led to the founding of Auburndale. Van Fleet came to Florida in 1877 with Alfred Parslow, who had received $10,000 from a railroad for injuries suffered in a train wreck in Ohio. With this capital the two men got a charter from Florida to start a railroad and built the first one through this section, from Kissimmee to Tampa and from Bartow Junction to Bartow in 1883.

After they had finished their railroad survey, Parslow and Van Fleet went home to Chicago and influenced Frank Fuller to return to Florida with them. Fuller and his father built a town between Kissimmee and Tampa and named it Sanitaria. The railroad wouldn't give them a station there but in 1887 located one a mile west with a post office and called it Auburndale. The town's name was supplied by Mrs. Pulsifer, wife of the publisher of the Boston Herald. Major Louis McLain, who supervised the building of the railroad in that area, wrote a glowing description of the place and asked the Pulsifers to give it a name. Mrs. Pulsifer picked Auburndale, the name of her hometown in Massachusetts.

Growth of the town proceeded well until 1911, when almost the entire business section was destroyed by fire. Services were being held in the Methodist church when a former town marshall suddenly appeared at the church door, raised his hand and called out, "Mr. Preacher, I don't want to interrupt your sermon, but the whole damn town is burning up."

Auburndale rebuilt after this disaster, but by 1940 the population had only reached 2,723. It jumped to 3,763 by 1950 and 5,593 by 1960. The 1980 census showed 6,501, and those who keep track of such matters expect the population to exceed 10,000 by the year 2000. In addition to the population growth, town administrators see a great potential for attracting more major industries to Auburndale. Meanwhile, home building proceeds at a steady pace. There were 55 building permits issued for homes and apartments in 1988.

The town plans to continue annexing the outlying areas by offering to extend the water and sewer lines to communities that vote to become part of the town.

Real estate costs are reasonable. Three-bedroom, two-bath homes with about 1,500 square feet of living space cost between $70,000 and $80,000. More expensive homes are also available, such as the 12 houses in one development in the $500,000 range plus quite a few others elsewhere in town in the $100,000 class. There are only a few condos and two mobile home parks. Mobile homes on a lake cost about $75,000. The millage rates are $3.68 in Auburndale and $10.66 in the county.

Here is a place that may leave the small town ranks sooner than many expected a few years ago, but the small town spirit is likely to endure much longer.

Clermont

Population 6,100. Central. 20 miles west of Orlando. Many retirees. Hospital, large library. Citrus wiped out by freeze, land being used for new homes. Very hilly area, many lakes in town and nearby. Some growth expected.

On Christmas morning in 1983 residents of central Florida awoke to one of the worst freezes in the 20th century. Temperatures dipped well below 20 degrees, and much of the richest citrus country in the state was devastated. Hundreds of thousands of orange and grapefruit trees were killed in a single night, and many growers were forced to abandon their groves.

No community was harder hit by this disaster of nature than Clermont, the Lake County town which calls itself the "Gem Of The Hills." In less than five years, though, Clermont rebounded to become one of the fastest growing towns in the area. Where thousands of acres of fruit trees grew up and down the scenic hills of this lake-dotted landscape, now large housing developments are taking their place. Fortunately, most of the developers are giving considerable attention to landscaping, so the change from citrus to houses is not so drastic that it threatens the natural beauty of the area.

Located only 20 miles west of booming Orlando and a half-hour drive from Walt Disney World, Clermont is attracting retirees as well as commuters in large numbers and could become the largest town in Lake County by the end of the century. From the air looking down, you wonder how they found room to build this town of 6,100 population. One sees large lakes in all directions, and the town appears to be a small island amidst all this water.

Clermont is probably the hilliest town in Florida, and all these hills combined with the lakes make it one of the state's most scenic spots. Luckily, the loss of the citrus trees didn't destroy the town's beauty since the giant oaks and other varieties of trees and plants weren't affected by the killer freeze.

In the surrounding countryside, almost 30 housing developments of varying sizes are being built. Many of them are designed for the affluent retirees, but those seeking less costly homes can find them. There is a wide range of prices. In Clermont, homes with two bedrooms and two baths average $50,000 to $60,000. The three-bedroom, two-bath homes, which predominate, are priced from $65,000 to $85,000. Townhouses with two bedrooms are about $55,000. Those favoring lakefront property will pay a 50 percent premium, and lots in this category are becoming scarce.

The town has been built around two major lakes, Lake Minneola and Lake Minnehaha, part of the Clermont Chain of Lakes, which includes 13 others. Most of these lakes are shallow (averaging 12 to 14 feet) with hard sandy bottoms. The pollution which has damaged so many of Florida's lakes has not invaded the Clermont area lakes, so all of them are available and used for recreation such as fishing, swimming, boating and waterskiing. Much of the water recreation is concentrated on Lake Minneola where there's a 1000-foot sandy beach, a city dock, a boat ramp and a 300-foot fishing pier.

A short distance south of Clermont is 1,790-acre Lake Louisa State Park. In the northeast corner of Florida's Green Swamp, it supplies much of the state's water supply. Large amounts of water accumulate here and filter down to replenish the underground limestone formations that provide Florida with its fresh water.

In addition to all the scenic beauty of the lakes and hills, the town also boasts two outstanding assets, a general cleanliness and good streets. Clermont takes great pride in both of these and has worked hard to achieve them. Very few towns are kept so tidy, and even fewer have such good streets.

Being so close to Orlando, the town has an unusual mix of retirees and commuters. Many of the residents found they could reach their jobs quicker at the large Martin Marietta plant in Orlando from Clermont than from many places in the Orlando metropolitan area. Others commute to jobs at Disney World and the other nearby attractions.

While the permanent population is 6,100, another 4,000 spend their winters here, many of whom escape the cold weather at Clerbrook Resort, an RV community about six miles north of Clermont. In the city limits is a manufactured housing development, Emerald Lakes, which has both permanent and winter-time residents.

Recreation isn't confined to the many lakes in Clermont. There's a nice 9-hole golf course in the city as well as an 18-hole course at Clerbrook, both open to the public. Just a few miles west of town is Green Valley Golf Course, a challenging par-72 layout.

The public tennis courts and shuffleboard facilities in a city park are very popular. For those who prefer to get their exercise from running, a jogging path goes around one of the lakes with exercise stations available along the route for users to monitor their heartbeat rates.

Shopping is divided between an older downtown section and a newer strip along State Road 50, where there's a good choice of supermarkets and other attractive businesses.

Living costs are not high. The millage rate is only $2.24 per $1,000 of assessed value for the city, plus $12.51 for the county.

Another asset is an outstanding public library. Located in a former bank building, it has a special reading room for seniors, a large selection of magazines and 45,000 books. There's no fee for residents and only $5 annually for visitors.

The town has a quality hospital, South Lake Memorial, which has 68 beds and serves the surrounding area.

Jenkins Auditorium, in the center of town is a community building used for a variety of functions, including wedding receptions, meetings of many of the town's 50 clubs, dancing and senior activities.

An active Art League in town, in operation since 1955, has

a permanent home in a building bought and refurbished to promote all the arts: crafts, poetry and prose as well as painting and sculpture.

Few towns in the state are changing as much as Clermont. When it celebrated its centennial in 1984 there had been no major changes in its history until the great Christmas freeze of 1983. Since then the area has experienced a metamorphosis of staggering proportions. Fortunately, it's something the town and surrounding area feel they can handle—beautifully!

DeBary

Population 6,500. Central. 25 miles north of Orlando. New town, started in 50s. Many retirees. St. Johns River three miles away, good fishing. Two large housing developments nearby. Unincorporated. Many job commuters.

One of Florida's newer small towns is DeBary, a community about 12 miles south of DeLand and 25 miles north of Orlando, built on the 19th-century estate of Count Samuel Frederick deBary.

A prominent wine importer from New York, deBary had been born in Germany of Belgian parents. As an avid sportsman interested in hunting and fishing, he had come to Florida in 1870 for a visit, been impressed with the area and built a wooden, two-story mansion in 1871. The building, called DeBary Hall, now belongs to the state of Florida and is used as a center for senior citizens.

DeBary's population in 1986 was 6,430, and projections call for 8,030 by the turn of the century. Census figures in 1980 listed the population as 4,980.

Despite being developed along both sides of busy U.S. Highway 17-92, the town is a quiet residential place attracting a good mix of age groups. While it was regarded in its early years as primarily a retirement community, many young families moved here in the 1980s, and 65 percent of the 1,200 children in a nearby elementary school are from DeBary. Only 38 percent of the population are 60 or over. The median age for the town is 48.

Like so many of these late blooming communities in Florida, this one is unincorporated. There are advantages to this unincorporated status, chief of which is no city tax. The millage rate for DeBary is $18.15 for each $1,000 of assessed value, all of which goes to the county. Since there is no city government in DeBary, all services for the town are provided by the county. This means most residents rely on the county to provide water, though some get theirs from individual wells. The county provides both police protection through a sheriff and fire protection. A modern and efficient fire station in the middle of the town assures there is no long wait after a fire has been reported. The county is also responsible for maintenance of the town's streets, most of which are paved.

Real estate prices in the community are not excessive, though more affluent house hunters can find accommodations well over $100,000.

In the part of the town that was first developed, houses with two bedrooms and two baths cost about $40,000, while those with three bedrooms are between $45,000 and $50,000. If you want to build your own home there, lots are about $8,000. New homes are being built for prices ranging between $80,000 and $100,000.

For those preferring manufactured housing, a development in a pretty setting along the St. Johns River includes homes with 1,586 square feet that cost about $40,000 and have two bedrooms and two baths. Smaller homes of 1,064 feet are $27,000. Both sized homes are built on lots that sell for $21,000 and measure about 75 by 100 feet. Larger lots are available.

At the north end of the town there is a country club resort community named Glen Abbey. It is a very desirable location, built in a wooded area around an 18-hole golf course. Two-bedroom villas there with 1,283 square feet cost $85,000 plus $40,000 for the lot. Three-bedroom villas with 1,447 square feet are $95,000. The villas offer all of the amenities, and monthly maintenance costs of $95 cover water, sewer, garbage and pest control services. Tennis and racquetball courts and a large pool are available for residents on a membership basis.

Also under construction is DeBary Plantation, another expensive but very attractive development where the lots are priced around $17,000, and the homes are in the $125,000 to $225,000 range. Plans there call for 1,458 homes to be constructed on 755 acres during a period from 1988 to 1998.

Because the town grew along the highway, there is no conventional small town business district. The town does, though, offer all the usual services and retail businesses. Just three miles away a new shopping center has an even greater selection.

Recreation facilities are plentiful. In addition to the golf course at Glen Abbey that is open to the public, a new 18-hole course will be ready in 1990 and two good courses in DeLand are available. There's a large public boat dock and good fishing on the scenic St. Johns River just three miles from the center of town. A short distance from the dock is a large community park, with softball diamonds, a soccer field and playground equipment for the small fry.

The closest hospitals are Central Florida Regional in Sanford, seven miles away, and Fish Memorial in DeLand.

Stetson University in DeLand offers a wide range of theatrical and musical programs during the school year.

DeBary has a town community center used extensively by a large variety of clubs and organizations for meetings and activities as well as for dances, both square and ballroom, which are held each week.

An attractive library of 2,400 square feet with over 10,000 books is open seven hours each Tuesday through Saturday.

Just five miles away is Blue Spring State park, noted as the winter gathering place of the manatee, large mammals that seek refuge here from the colder water of the St. Johns River from November through April. Visitors to the park also use scenic Blue Spring Run for canoeing and swimming in water that is 72 degrees the year-round.

The town has no schools, but county buses transport the kids to Deltona for middle school and high school and to

Enterprise for elementary school.

DeBary Hall is in daily use by the Volusia County Council on Aging. Hot meals are served there each weekday noon for those over 60, and other meals are provided by Meals on Wheels. Counseling services for the seniors are also offered.

DeBary is in a rural setting, but the bright lights are not far away. It's a half-hour drive on Interstate 4 to Orlando, and Daytona Beach, in the same county, is just as close.

The pace here is slow. Many of the residents commute to jobs in Orlando and Daytona Beach, and the young families have been assimilated with the retirees to make it a typical Florida small town. The town has a five-year plan that includes discussion of eventual incorporation. There is no rush, though. The wheels turn slowly here, and most of the residents seem to prefer it that way.

Eustis

Population 13,000. Central. 35 miles northwest of Orlando. Many retirees. On large lake, good fishing. Community college. Citrus wiped out by freeze. New industries provide jobs. Large hospital. Pretty town.

Like so many other towns in the midsection of Florida, Eustis was hard hit by the devastating Christmas freeze of 1983. And like the others, this town has bounced back to become one of the most prosperous communities in the state.

Dead citrus groves surround the town on three sides. On the fourth side is Lake Eustis, seven miles long and five miles wide. One of Florida's larger lakes, it is also one of its cleanest.

In the five years since the killer freeze, retail trade employment has increased by 41 percent, and services have provided over 35 percent more jobs. When the citrus industry went out of business, many jobs were lost. In the last three years, though, the unemployment rate has dropped from 11 percent to five percent, due in part to industries like Florida

Foods, which creates aloe for cosmetics industries around the world, Mercer Plastics and Electron Machine Corp.

Eustis was incorporated in 1883, and in the years since has become one of the state's prettiest towns. The population was 9,453 in 1980 and is estimated over 13,000 now. Shaded streets predominate in the quiet residential sections of the town, and the owners take great pride in well-tended lawns and flower gardens.

The business section developed along the lakefront and expanded to an area along U.S. Highway 441. The big supermarkets and shopping centers are located there, while the smaller businesses are concentrated in the older downtown area. Two streets in this section have been redone and are referred to as The Village. No auto traffic is allowed on these streets where pedestrians enjoy brick sidewalks and tree shaded benches.

One business downtown, Ferran's, has been in Eustis since 1884, and a sign outside proclaims it as "The Store With Squeaky Floors." A well stocked department store, it still retains a flavor of its earlier days, small stools at the dry goods counter for the ladies to sit on while going through the patterns for their next sewing project.

Towering over the downtown area is Waterman Hospital. It's an unusually large hospital for a town of this size, 182 beds, a staff of 55 and all the services offered by large city hospitals. Because it serves 23,000 patients annually, the major employment category in Eustis is medical and health care services.

The Waterman name comes from Frank Waterman, the head of the Waterman Fountain Pen Company in New York. Impressed with Eustis during winter stays here, he built a big hotel in the early 1920s, appropriately named the Fountain Inn, which did well until the Depression years. After the hotel was forced to close, Waterman gave the building to the city for a hospital.

Living costs in Eustis are on the reasonable side. The tax millage is $6.0, plus $12.5 for the county. The median cost for a three-bedroom, two-bath house is $65,000, well below the national average. Apartments of two bedrooms and one bath rent for about $350 per month, while those with three bedrooms and two baths run about $450 to $500 per month.

An estimated 40 percent of the population is retired, most of whom have migrated from the Midwest states of Indiana, Ohio, Wisconsin and Michigan. Many Eustis residents are commuters, at least 20 to 25 percent driving to jobs in neighboring Seminole and Orange Counties. Orlando is only 35 miles away. All the traffic isn't one way, though, since about 12 percent of the working force commutes from Orange and Seminole to jobs in Eustis.

Many recreation facilities are available for all age groups. There are a couple dozen lighted shuffleboard courts, tennis courts and several handball and racquetball courts next to a recently constructed senior center. Ferran Park on the lakefront has more shuffleboard courts, a jogging trail, a heated swimming pool and a bandshell. The Community Center provides playing fields for soccer, basketball and softball.

Many fishermen keep active on a daily basis at Lake Eustis, which gets heavy use at all times of the year. There are three public boat ramps there, a large swimming area with a sandy beach and picnic tables open to the public at all times.

There's only one golf course in Eustis, the 18-hole Pine Meadows Country Club. It's private, but there are many more courses nearby that are open to the public.

For hunters and hikers the sprawling Ocala National Forest is only 20 minutes north of Eustis.

At the senior center, in addition to the sports facilities, there's a busy schedule of other activities, including courses in ceramics, caning, basketry, quilting and cameo painting. Bridge, table games, bingo and a variety of music programs also are offered for the seniors.

Prospective students can choose from a wide selection of subjects at a variety of schools. Within a 35-mile radius of Eustis there are four major colleges and universities. The immediate vicinity has two well-above-average schools, Lake Sumter Community College and Lake County Vo-Tech. Lake Sumter ranks among the top three community colleges in the state and offers 41 subject areas ranging from art and business to real estate and speech. Many retirees take advantage of the opportunities there for continuing their education. The Vo-Tech Center is a specialized post-secondary institution that provides job preparatory training.

The local high school is not without its claims to fame, having produced Nobel Prize winner Robert Shrieffer in physics and astronaut David Walker.

In the older part of the business section, near the lake, an old movie theater has been converted into a place for stage productions, where the Bay Street Players have become a talented amateur theatrical group. Now in their 14th season, the players put on seven productions each year along with three full-scale musicals.

The Eustis Art League is active from October to April and puts on several exhibits annually. For most residents of Eustis, as well as the surrounding area, the premier event of the year is the George Washington Birthday Festival, the oldest continuous festival in Florida. There were just a few bicycles and Model-T cars in the first one in 1902, but it has since become a major production with a giant parade of floats, marching bands and drill units, an arts and craft exhibit, a patriotic essay contest, races and a big fireworks show.

Eustis also established a library in 1902, now the oldest in the county. In an attractive building formerly occupied by a supermarket, it houses 52,000 books and 1,000 records, film-strips, periodicals and cassettes for adults and children.

Next to the Community Center on Lake Eustis is a stately two-story mansion, the Clifford Taylor House, built in 1910 and 1911. A historical museum since 1975, it has been preserved close to its original state, including a cast iron kitchen sink first used in 1876.

It's been a long time since the days when the railroad engineers blew long blasts on their locomotive whistles to warn farmers of freezing weather so they could protect the citrus trees and other crops from frost. The population has doubled in less than 20 years and is expected to double again in 15 more. Even with this growth, Eustis maintains its small town atmosphere. It's a very desirable place to raise a family.

Frostproof

Population 3,300. Central. 70 miles south of Orlando. Many retirees. Citrus dominates area. Two citrus plants in town. Outstanding library. Community college nearby. Two large lakes New high school.

There is, not surprisingly, only one town in the U.S. named Frostproof, and it's located in central Florida amidst some of the world's richest citrus producing areas. It's in Polk County, which boasts the distinction of producing more oranges and grapefruit than all of the state of California.

Here is a town totally dominated by citrus, surrounded as it is by thousands of acres of groves. Two major citrus plants are located in the town. The nearest four-lane highway is several miles away, so visitors to Frostproof arrive on lightly traveled roads. Although the town is somewhat isolated, the lack of traffic and noise has been attracting retirees in increasing numbers.

An old depot houses the chamber of commerce, Frostproof, Polk County, the biggest citrus producing county in the U.S.

For those seeking a quiet spot with most of the amenities and easy access to the larger cities of Florida this would be a good choice. The town is squeezed between two pretty lakes, Clinch Lake on the west and Lake Reedy on the east. There are nice residential sections, a prosperous looking business section, an attractive new library, an impressive new high school building and residents who seem to take pride in their town. The streets are paved, and the homes are in good condition with well-tended lawns and flower gardens.

Although the population now is about 3,300, the town grew very slowly in its early years. As recently as 1923 it was less than 1,000 and only 1,500 by 1936.

Frostproof is located on the former site of Fort Clinch, an outpost established during the Indian wars of 1849–1858. The first house in the area was a log cabin, constructed in the 1880s. By 1900, there were only 30 people living there. In the earliest days, Frostproof was known as Keystone City, but a town named Keystone Heights in north Florida was causing some confusion, so Keystone City was changed to Lakemont in 1898.

A man named Joseph Washington Carson is generally credited with naming the town Frostproof. After all the fruit was lost by a killer freeze in December 1894, another freeze two months later caused most fruit trees in northern Florida to split right down to the ground. In Frostproof, though, residents pruned their trees, sawing off dead limbs and most of the tops. The trees responded by blooming again within a month and bore fruit later that year.

Carson, on hearing about the tree damage in north Florida, made a trip to Orlando and other citrus areas north of Lakemont and was amazed at the total destruction. When he returned, he said, "We've got the name for this place now. It's Frostproof."

By 1906 the name was officially changed from Lakemont to Frostproof, and by 1918 the residents had approved incorporation.

Even in recent years the town's somewhat unusual name has proved appropriate. Another devastating freeze hit in 1962, and temperatures were well below freezing all over

Florida. But in Frostproof the thermometer didn't go as low or stay there as long, and the trees suffered no damage.

Living in Frostproof in the early years of this century was something of a challenge. Modern conveniences were unknown, and people scratched out a living from the land. In 1903, Frostproof had no post office, so a man carried the mail by bicycle from Bartow to Frostproof, a round trip of 56 miles, six days a week for an annual salary of $495. He left Bartow at 7:30 A.M. and returned at 7:30 P.M., making the entire trip over sandy trails.

Many people invested in land around Frostproof after the trees survived several freezes, and by 1912 the railroad had arrived. The town grew gradually and has continued at that pace since.

That the town has grown to its present size and prospered is due primarily to two giants of the citrus industry. One was Latt Maxcy, who moved here from Fort Meade in 1904 and opened a large citrus plant. One of the pioneers in the citrus industry, he played a major role in Florida's emergence as the country's largest producer of oranges and grapefruit. The other giant is Ben Hill Griffin Jr., Maxcy's nephew who created a massive empire of citrus, cattle and land and is one of the richest men in America.

Both men achieved large fortunes by virtue of hard work and shrewd business operations. And neither forgot his roots. Maxcy lived in Frostproof until his death, and Griffin lives only a few miles away. In 1988 Forbes magazine listed his fortune as $300 million.

Griffin started out working in his uncle's fruit packing house pushing a floor truck for 15 cents an hour. He later ran a fertilizer plant for his uncle before entering the cattle business in 1941. By then he had acquired some grove property of his own and continued to expand his holdings. By 1953 he had taken over a canning operation, and in 1958 he bought the Minute Maid processing plant in Frostproof previously owned by his uncle. In 1981, Proctor and Gamble bought Griffin's plant, though he continued to supply fruit for this operation. Later Griffin started his own fresh fruit shipping business nearby, which he still operates. P&G employs about

500 people, and Griffin's operation employs another 200, so it's not hard to understand what Maxcy and Griffin have meant to Frostproof.

No town in the state is more citrus oriented than Frostproof. In addition to the two large plants owned by P&G and Griffin, there are some lush groves right in the town. Griffin owns several thousand acres of citrus, but many other people in the area have made sizable fortunes from raising fruit as well.

Since the town's only movie theater closed several years ago, and there are no active art or drama groups, most cultural activities center around the schools, churches and families.

Much of the recreational activity is concentrated in the two lakes bordering the town. The residents use both for boating and fishing, and Clinch Lake has a mile and a half beach for swimming plus picnic facilities.

When the new high school was built, the old school was turned into the city hall, so the gym there is used by the town's recreation department. Nearby there are four softball diamonds, handball courts and a game room. The nearest golf course is a 9-hole layout just a few minutes from town. Near downtown there are three tennis courts and a playground for children. Next to Lake Reedy is a Tourist Club that has ten shuffleboard courts and is used heavily by the town's retirees, who constitute about half the population.

Many of the retirees live in mobile home parks in Frostproof, and several more such parks are just outside the town. Conventional homes with three bedrooms and two baths run about $50,000; many homes in the $100,000-plus range have been built near Clinch Lake. The town's tax millage rate is $4. Living costs are low, and the water and sewer fees are well below the average. Though Frostproof is without a hospital, the town supplies ambulance service to two large and well staffed ones a few miles away in Lake Wales and Avon Park.

With all that fruit to be picked for market, the need for workers becomes great in the fall, when about 2,000 to 3,000 migrants, mostly Mexicans, arrive. They stay until about Easter and live in trailer parks in the area. These workers, plus the many retirees who are here just during the winter, double the population for three or four months. Unemployment is not a problem at most times and is usually under five percent, except during cutbacks at the citrus plants in the summer.

In addition to the citrus plants, there is other evidence of the Maxcy and Griffin influence. Near downtown is the Latt Maxcy Memorial Library, built in 1978 by the Latt Maxcy Foundation and housing 25,000 volumes.

Mr. Griffin has been generous in many projects in Frostproof through the years. He recently purchased the old Seaboard Coastline depot and adjoining park and leased them to the city for $1 per year. The depot is now used by the chamber of commerce. In 1988 he supplied money for an addition to the Frostproof museum.

Shopping facilities in town are adequate, but major items must be purchased a short distance away in Lakeland, Winter Haven and Lake Wales.

Many graduates of the local high school continue their education at community colleges nearby in Winter Haven and Avon Park, both of which offer adult education courses.

The city, hemmed in as it is by the two lakes, has no plans for any further annexation. There's still room for more residents in the town, and retirees will continue finding their way here to enjoy the quiet life-style of Frostproof.

Lake Wales

Population 9,000. Central. 70 miles east of Tampa. Citrus producing area. Several citrus plants in town. Downtown recently restored. Part of Florida Main Street program. Bok Tower. Many lakes. Two colleges nearby.

Unlike many Florida towns and cities that grew in all directions with little or no planning, Lake Wales was well thought out from its beginning. Fortunately, for the 9,000 citizens liv-

One of the world's greatest carillons, fifty-three bells ring out from Bok Tower across the rolling hills of Lake Wales.

ing here, the planning hasn't stopped. While many cities around the U.S. have despaired of saving their downtown areas, Lake Wales has taken important steps to greatly improve its own.

The Florida Main Street program, launched in 1985, was designed to revive the downtown areas around the state, and 18 cities had participated by 1988. Since Lake Wales got involved in 1987, the change here has been dramatic. Old and decaying store fronts have been restored, new sidewalks installed, shrubs and plants added throughout the area and interiors of many businesses modernized to give the entire downtown section an amazingly new appearance.

Lake Wales is deservedly referred to as "The Crown Jewel of the Ridge." The city lies among gently rolling hills covered with citrus trees on the highest ground in the entire Florida peninsula—250 feet above sea level.

In 1983 a quirk of nature smiled on Lake Wales. While just 50 miles away hundreds of thousands of citrus trees were killed by the terrible Christmas freeze, Lake Wales and the nearby surrounding area escaped with only minor damage.

Citrus was king here before the Christmas freeze and still is. The largest employer in Lake Wales is Citrus World, processor of the famous Donald Duck products. Over 700 people are employed there on a regular basis, while several hundred more work at the smaller citrus packing firms. There are other plants in town, including a mattress manufacturer that employs over 100.

Tourism also is a major business in the area, with Bok Tower, the Passion Play and Spook Hill each attracting thousands of visitors each year. The stately Bok Tower is the highest elevation on the peninsula at 295 feet and houses one of the world's great carillons with 53 bells ranging from 17 pounds to nearly 12 tons in weight. At Spook Hill, one of the state's more unusual attractions, you can drive your car to a designated spot. Put the car in neutral and take your foot off the brake. The car will then mysteriously begin to move slowly backwards and uphill.

The Black Hills Passion Play, portraying the final week of Christ's life on earth, has been presented annually since 1952 from mid-February to the middle of April at an amphitheater two miles south of Lake Wales.

For the baseball fans, and there are thousands of them in the area every March, three major league teams train in Polk County each spring. The Detroit Tigers are at Lakeland, the Boston Red Sox at Winter Haven and the Kansas City Royals near Haines City, all within a short drive of Lake Wales.

This is a town which hasn't experienced spectacular growth, despite all its assets. The population was 5,000 in 1928, and is only 9,000 now. About 25 percent of these are retirees, mostly from the Midwest. Another 300 Canadians spend their winters here, and there are 25,000 other residents within ten miles. Folks who live here say they like the town being small enough to be friendly. Life moves at a slower pace, but it's not far to the bright lights. Tampa and Orlando are only an hour away.

Soon after the incorporation of the town in 1911, the residents built a $500,000 hotel with 100 rooms. An impressive, 11-story structure, it towers above the town and is visible for miles in all directions. It's well preserved and still operating, though its name has been changed from the original Dixie Walesbilt to the Hotel Grand.

When the early planners laid out Lake Wales, they didn't neglect the green areas. There are many parks and recreation facilities on over 200 city acres, including nine tennis courts, seven city parks, a bike and hike trail, a community center, two racquetball courts, a public boat ramp and 12 ball fields.

The Tourist Club, built in 1940, provides 24 lighted shuffleboard courts and several lawn bowling greens. An Olympic sized pool at the Y is open from April through October.

For the golfers there's the 6,300-yard Lake Wales Country Club, while several municipal and other public courses are available for greens fees within a short drive of the town.

The fisherman have a wide choice of lakes for snaring black bass, speckled perch, bream, bluegill and catfish. Catches of bass weighing nine and ten pounds are not uncommon. Lake Cooper is supposed to be the best spot.

While there is a good selection of condominiums and apartments for sale or rent, reasonably priced homes are also available. A three-bedroom, two-bath home usually costs about $70,000. One development in the city has smaller homes for $60,000. A development outside the city has 150 homes in the $80,000 to $90,000 bracket. The tax millage is $5.5 for the city and $10.66 for the county.

Two small colleges just south of the city offer a good choice of courses. Webber College at Babson Park specializes in business courses, including hotel management, while Warner Southern is a Christian liberal arts school that provides special training for missionary work in third-world countries. Adult education classes are available at the high school and Ridge Vo-Tech.

An attractive library, built in 1960, has 38,000 volumes and has scheduled a $250,000 expansion. It's open six days a week.

The Arts Council is in charge of cultural activities in the city and serves as a liaison between arts and dramatic groups, galleries and other organizations. It sponsors an annual lakeside Lake Wales Art Show. There's an active Lake Wales Little Theater and Children's Theater.

Health facilities are excellent for a city of this size. The Lake Wales Hospital, fully equipped, has 154 beds plus another 120 beds in an extended care unit for outpatients.

While the revived downtown shopping area is a busy place, the big supermarkets, fast food franchises and some other large stores are out on U.S. Highway 27 and S.R. 60.

Next to the towering Hotel Grand, the easiest building to spot in Lake Wales is the Depot Museum, formerly the Atlantic Coast Line depot. Local history buffs took it over when the railroad stopped running and have created a highly interesting collection of memorabilia about the area's past. It opened on July 4, 1976, and nobody has trouble locating it since the exterior is a very bright pink with white trim.

It all adds up to a pretty town with an enviable life-style. Lake Wales residents are not interested in booming growth. They just want to maintain their town as a neat place to live.

Mount Dora

Population 6,000. Central. 30 miles northwest of Orlando. 60 percent of population retired. Town looks like New England. Many antique shops. On large lake, many other lakes nearby. Yacht Club. Boating, fishing big.

Except for the palm trees and Spanish moss, you might assume you're entering a typical town in New England when you arrive in Mount Dora. Nestled among the lakes and hills of Lake County in central Florida, here is one of the state's prettiest towns.

Sixty percent of the 6,000 population are retirees, most from the northeast and Midwest. New England accents are not uncommon here.

Stately old homes, some even dating back to the 19th century, well-kept lawns, an abundance of large oak trees and a prosperous looking business section combine to make you feel you're somewhere in Maine. The town is built on a bluff about 185 feet above Lake Dora, a picture postcard setting.

Much of the housing is expensive, but other living costs are not out of line. Condominiums are priced at $100,000 and up, while town houses are considerably more. A few mobile-modular homes in the $50,000 bracket are available, and some folks buy small but older homes for around $50,000 and renovate them. Rentals are not plentiful. A large development of 600 houses is planned just east of the town and will be annexed. This is expected to add about 1,800 people to the population. Most of the homes will be in the $85,000 to $135,000 range.

The millage rate for Mount Dora is $6.2 for each $1,000 of assessed value, plus $12.51 for each $1,000 for the county, a total of $18.71.

Shopping is never a problem. Two large grocery chains have supermarkets in the town, and Eustis, only three miles away, offers a good variety of stores. Also, Orlando is only 25 miles down the road.

If you're in the market for antiques, you'll never have to leave Mount Dora. There are over a dozen antique shops in the town, and all of them are well stocked.

That over half the population is retired is not surprising in light of the many activities that are available. The many shuf-

Masonic temple is representative of the postcard-pretty, New England charm of Mount Dora.

fleboard and lawn bowling facilities attract enough competitors to keep them busy on a year-round basis, members paying only a minimal fee for their use. Tennis courts and racquetball courts also are open to the public, along with a municipal swimming pool that is heated and open all year. There is only one golf course in Mount Dora, an 18-hole semi-private layout, but there are many other 9-hole and 18-hole courses within a short distance of the town.

For those concerned about cultural activities, Mount Dora boasts one of the best amateur theater groups in Florida, the Ice House Players. Now in their 40th year, the players put on seven productions yearly, and many of those attending drive in from Orlando. The Mount Dora Center for the Arts offers year-round activities for both youth and adults.

Boating enthusiasts will not be disappointed in Mount Dora. In fact, many of those living there were first attracted by the boating possibilities. There are lakes in all directions, over 1,400 in Lake County, and many of them are connected. Mount Dora is on a chain of lakes, and it's possible, by using the Dora Canal and other canals and locks, to steer your boat all the way from Mount Dora to the Inland Waterway and the Atlantic Ocean. One enterprising boater likes to tell how he took his boat from Mount Dora to Jacksonville on the Atlantic, down to the Florida Keys, into the Gulf of Mexico, through the Panama Canal, then to the Pacific, ending up in San Diego.

The major lakes in the area are Lake Dora, Lake Eustis, Lake Harris and Little Lake Harris, all good for fishing and boating. Most boaters prefer cruising those lakes to trips to San Diego. For yacht enthusiasts, an impressive Yacht Club on Lake Dora recently celebrated its 75th year. The oldest yacht club in inland Florida, it sponsors the annual Mount Dora Sailing Regatta in April.

While the town is usually quiet and off the beaten path, there are a few occasions when Mount Dora gets crowded. Each February it hosts the Mount Dora Art Festival, and crowds up to 150,000 pour in for two days. About 300 artists display their works, making this the second largest central Florida art show. In October about 1,500 bicycle riders converge on the town for the Mount Dora Bicycle Festival and spend three days exploring the countryside on a variety of rides ranging from ten to 100 miles. Also in October, there is a crafts show and the Dora Invitational Golf Tournament.

A recent addition to Mount Dora has been the 36,000 volume public library that is open daily except Sunday. It's well above average and caters to all ages.

Local clubs and organizations don't lack for meeting places. The Mount Dora Chamber of Commerce took over the railroad depot when passenger service was discontinued several years ago, and offers a meeting room there with kitchen facilities. In addition, the town has an attractive community building that seats 700 in its auditorium and is fully air conditioned. Kitchen facilities are also available there, and the building is in great demand at all times of the year for various functions.

While Mount Dora does not have a hospital, a 182-bed medical center is available in nearby Eustis, offering a 24-hour emergency room, intensive care and coronary care. The medical staff includes 55 physicians.

Water for the town is obtained from wells and is treated by chlorination. Also on the plus side is a state-of-the-art sewage plant that is the only one in central Florida reusing all the effluent. The water is used in sprinklers in city parks, on school grounds and city property.

Mount Dora's slogan, "Escape to Yesterday," is used extensively by the chamber of commerce in promoting the town as a throwback to a quieter era. In all of Florida there probably is no more laid-back town than Mount Dora. U.S. Highway 441, one of Florida's busiest roads, used to go right down the main business street of the town. Then, about 30 years ago, the highway needed to be four-laned as the traffic increased, and the folks in Mount Dora persuaded the state road officials to reroute 441 to bypass their town. Most cities want the increased business that more traffic brings, but Mount Dora wanted to enjoy the peace and quiet on Lake Dora and eliminate the endless drone of heavy traffic through its streets.

Here is a town not courting new industries, not interested in any record-breaking growth. It has NOT ONE fast-food restaurant. The people here remember how it used to be, and they are doing their level best to keep it that way.

Orange City

*Population 4,000 Central. 35 miles north of Orlando.
St. Johns River two miles away, good fishing, boating.
Blue Spring State Park nearby. Four miles to Stetson
University. Many retirees. Gradual growth.*

As growth creeps up on three sides of Orange City, this Volusia
County town still manages to remain separate from all the
various developments and towns that keep inching toward it.

Located in the western part of the county, a half-hour's drive
from Daytona Beach, Orange City will eventually adjoin
DeLand to the north. Less than four miles apart both towns
continue to add houses and businesses at a pace that may put
them side by side in another decade.

DeLand, the county seat of Volusia, is a small city of about
20,000. Orange City, meanwhile, places its population at
4,000 and doesn't anticipate the addition of any large numbers
of new residents in the years ahead.

Growth is not a dirty word in Orange City, but the town is
not interested in a population boom. It's a small town with a
great deal of community pride and a desire to maintain the
slow-paced life-style of the last century.

U.S. Highway 17-92 goes right through the middle of Orange
City, and the town has grown up on both sides of it. The
businesses hug the highway, and the houses, many of them
going back to the 19th century, are situated along the shaded
streets. Most are well maintained with neat lawns and lots of
flowers. Norman Rockwell could have used much of the town
as a model for his *Saturday Evening Post* covers.

Orange City is one of several towns developed along the St.
Johns River on its northward course to the Atlantic Ocean at
Jacksonville. The river is just two miles west of the town.
Residents and visitors spend many hours there in their boats
as they soak up the scenery or try their luck at fishing.

The river brought the settlers to Orange City, and the first
one was Louis Thursby. He and his wife arrived in 1856, built
a log cabin at Blue Spring, and lived there until a three-story

frame house was completed in 1872. Constructed on shell mounds left by the Timucuan Indians through the centuries, the house still overlooks Blue Spring, now a state park. Nearby are old pilings of a steamboat dock that was used when crops were brought to the river for shipment to Jacksonville and other points further north.

A group of six men from Wisconsin arrived in the area in 1876 and bought several thousand acres at $1.25 an acre, which they later sold at a neat profit to settlers who developed the site of the present Orange City. The previous year a small hotel had been built in Orange City by H.H. DeYarman. The building has been added to through the years but is still being used on the main business street.

By 1882 the organization of Orange City had been approved, and seven years later the city's charter was approved by the state. In the years since, the town has grown very gradually. Since it's just off Interstate 4, midway between Orlando and Daytona Beach, those seeking a taste of city life don't have a long drive.

The town has no industry, so many of the residents either commute to jobs in DeLand, Daytona Beach and Orlando or rely on service jobs to make a living. About 40 percent of the population is retired, having migrated here from the north or other areas of Florida. Several residents moved here from Daytona Beach and Orlando to escape the noise and congestion of those tourist-oriented cities.

Blue Spring State Park is the leading attraction in the area. Just outside Orange City it draws large crowds when the manatees seek shelter from the colder waters of the Atlantic from November to April. The temperature in Blue Spring is a constant 72 degrees, and about 25 manatees winter there each year. Each one has a known history, having been tracked for several years. The creatures survive only in Florida but once ranged as far away as Texas and North Carolina. The manatees aren't the only ones using the spring, since both swimmers and canoeists enjoy it at all times of the year.

For those preferring their recreation on land, there are two fine 18-hole golf courses at nearby housing developments. In the town, Valentine Park is the major recreation center with facilities that include two lighted tennis courts, a lighted basketball court, soccer and baseball fields and pavilions for cookouts. In the center of town is the Shuffleboard Club with 16 lighted courts for the older folks.

There's only an elementary school in Orange City, so the older kids go to a new high school in the big Deltona development nearby. In the area there is a wide choice of colleges. Stetson University is next door in DeLand, while the University of Central Florida, Valencia Community College and Rollins College are only 35 miles away in the Orlando metro area. Sanford has another community college just a 15-minute drive from Orange City. Bethune Cookman College and Embry Riddle Aeronautical University are in Daytona Beach. All offer adult education courses.

Orange City has had a library since 1918, when the Dickinson Memorial Library was built. Expanded in 1984 it has 10,000 volumes.

The town has no active art group, but a very ambitious Theater Center, Inc. will soon be moving into a new $4.6 million center cross from Stetson. This group puts on seven or eight productions per year and also performs about 65 times each year for school groups in the area, entertaining nearly 75,000 children in the last five years.

The biggest annual event staged in Orange City each year is the Manatee Festival. Held the last weekend in January at Valentine Park and Blue Spring, it includes an arts and crafts show, a beauty pageant and live entertainment.

While Orange City doesn't have a hospital, there are three major ones a few minutes away with a combined total of over 300 beds. Central Florida Regional Medical Center is in Sanford, while DeLand has Fish Memorial Hospital and West Volusia Memorial Hospital.

Until recent years shopping facilities in Orange City had been somewhat limited. Now there are two very large shopping centers in town, located in what is known as the Four Townes area, where Orange City, Deltona, DeBary and the historic town of Enterprise converge. The big supermarket chains are there along with a wide variety of other stores.

Only 1,598 in 1960, the population has more than doubled

since, due largely to developments popping up in Orange City. The largest of these is Country Village, an attractive community of about 1,200 residents built around one of the 18-hole golf courses mentioned earlier. It's in a heavily wooded area since the only trees removed were those making room for the streets and manufactured homes. Closer to the main part of town is Orange Tree Village, another manufactured home development that includes a swimming pool, clubhouse and other amenities.

Just outside Orange City is John Knox Village, a well planned development of 700 people that offers nine different floor plans. It's expensive but offers far more services than similar operations.

The main part of town has a mix of older homes and new models, and those on the market are reasonably priced. The tax millage rate is $5.89 in town and $16 in the county.

At first glance Orange City almost seems to be a throwback to the Florida small towns of 50 years ago, when the pace was much slower than today's. On closer examination, though, it appears in tune with the times but still not interested in any expansion. The population projections call for only 4,300 in 1990 and 5,700 by 2000, reasonable figures for the local residents. Most are not in favor of any annexation and would prefer to keep the town at its present size. Even with the encroachments of the various nearby developments, it's unlikely Orange City will leave the small town ranks soon.

St. Cloud

Population 9,000. Central. 21 miles south of Orlando, near Disney World. Many retirees. On large lake. Good recreational, cultural facilities. Hospital. Community college. Three industries.

Today Walt Disney World and the wonders of Epcot are only a half-hour away, but in the late 19th century, what is now

St. Cloud was part of a vast plantation. A Philadelphia manufacturer named Hamilton Disston bought four million acres of land for raising sugar and rice in Central Florida in 1881 for 25 cents an acre. The site of his huge sugar plant eventually became the town of St. Cloud.

When Disston's sugar and rice venture didn't pan out, he switched to citrus, lumber and cattle, all of which are still a source of income in this area. The town acquired its name from one of Disston's engineers, a native of St. Cloud, France.

St. Cloud was established by the Seminole Land and Investment Company in 1909 as a retirement community for Civil War veterans. For just $50, the first settlers each received a 25 x 125 foot city lot, a five-acre tract outside of town and a share of stock in the Colony Company. The price later jumped to $100, but in the first year this generous offer attracted over 2,000 people.

By the time St. Cloud was incorporated in 1911, it had adopted the nickname "Home of the Friendly Soldier." Reveille was blown in the morning and taps at night.

From that unusual beginning in the early part of the 20th century, St. Cloud experienced steady growth as retirees found this quiet town in Osceola County, just 21 miles south of Orlando. It was still only about 5,000 population in 1970, but the years that followed brought spectacular changes to the area. Walt Disney World opened in 1971, and St. Cloud, Osceola County and all of central Florida would never be quite the same again.

Even with Disney, however, and its millions of tourists St. Cloud itself has not been drastically altered. Cattle ranchers in cowboy boots and wide-brimmed hats are still a common sight, and the retirees are very much in evidence.

The population mix has changed some since the Disney arrival. While the retirees were predominant 20 years ago, the median age is now 45, and large numbers of young couples have been moving into the town. Proof of this is the recent addition of two elementary schools. Most of the retirees have come from New England and other northeastern states. Many of the young folks that have been moving in commute to jobs at Disney or at tourist-related businesses nearby.

Disney doesn't dominate St. Cloud as it does its neighboring town of Kissimmee, the Osceola County seat, 10 miles away. Mercury Marine, a division of Brunswick Corp., has nearly 400 employees at a plant in St. Cloud, and two firms making precast concrete and satellite antennas hire another 125.

Now that the population has approached 10,000, St. Cloud has kept pace with the growth by greatly improving the life-style for all its residents. The town is still laid-back, but it hasn't neglected those amenities which can make small-town living such a pleasant experience.

St. Cloud has developed along the shores of East Lake To-hopekaliga, a large body of water heavily used by boaters and fishermen. Built in a marina on the lake, a public boat basin provides easy access. Nearby a sandy beach is available for swimming.

The town fans out from this lake in a neatly laid out grid of streets. Most of the latter are paved, and many of the sandy ones are scheduled for paving soon. Like so many other Florida towns, the new and larger businesses have moved to a major highway, in this case U.S. Highway 192-441, which bisects the entire town. The older businesses and small shops are still in the downtown area.

Get on that major highway and you can be at the gates of Disney in a half-hour if you have good luck with the traffic lights through and beyond Kissimmee.

While the cost of living in St. Cloud is lower than many Florida towns, real estate is slightly higher than the average, probably due to the proximity of Disney and Orlando.

Most of the older houses in St. Cloud are of frame construction and are not costly, though many require some renovation. The concrete block homes are newer and cost more. On the edge of town is Pine Lake Estates, an exclusive residential development in business since the early days of Disney. About 300 homes have been built there, ranging in cost from $80,000 to $170,000. For those seeking low-cost housing there are two mobile home parks.

The city supplies both electric power and water at reasonable rates. Ad valorum taxes are not high, less than $5 per $1,000 for the city and about $12 for the county.

Medical facilities are well above the average. The huge Orlando Regional Medical Center operates a branch hospital in St. Cloud with 84 beds, 24-hour emergency room service, radiology, surgery and a cardiac care unit.

The attractive senior center is a busy place, serving as the meeting place for 92 clubs and serving 60 to 100 lunches daily.

A town library operates from a building downtown, but a new 48,000 square foot building has been approved and will be part of the Osceola County library system. The present library has 30,000 volumes, but the residents also have free access to the Orange County system and its 693,000 volumes.

A wide variety of entertainment is offered throughout the year. The Rotary Club sponsors a "spring fling" that attracts crowds of more than 25,000 for boat races on Lake Tohopekaliga. The largest rodeo in Florida is staged on grounds between St. Cloud and Kissimmee each February and July with residents of both towns taking part.

Just outside the town is the Osceola Center for the Arts that houses an historical museum, a genealogy group, theater group and art gallery. The Osceola Players stage five productions each year, and the art gallery has eight exhibits annually, including an international one. The Popcorn Players, for children 8 to 16, also put on programs, and a Young Adults Chorus, for those 18 to 35, presents two programs yearly.

Recreation facilities are plentiful and include a Civic Center with recreation gym, two lighted softball fields, a Little League field and a senior league field, also lighted. At a Community House there are 24 shuffleboard courts and nine horseshoe pits, all lighted. Along with the swimming beach and marina on the lakefront is a 2½-mile exercise-bicycle path. Lighted tennis courts and handball-racquetball courts are in Godwin Park, over half of which is a natural pine forest.

Out near the rodeo grounds is a branch of Valencia Community College, which is based in Orlando. This new facility has a continuing education program that includes business courses, a computer school and real estate classes as well as classes in such diverse subjects as chemistry, geology, humanities, journalism, political science and Spanish.

This is a town which has undergone major changes in less

than two decades. It has avoided getting engulfed by the mushrooming growth generated by Disney and retained its small town flavor. Although keeping pace with the growth since Disney arrived, it has no ambitions to become a boomtown.

Tavares

Population 7,000. Central. 30 miles northwest of Orlando. On large lake, many others nearby. Over half of population is retired. Many mobile homes. Historical museum. Community college nearby. Four industries. Some growth expected.

Fishing and boating are major activities in Lake County, and no town there is closer to the water than Tavares. Most of the town of 7,000 is built on a narrow strip of land between Lake Dora and Lake Eustis.

Tavares is the county seat of Lake County, an area that was one of the leading producers of citrus in Florida before a Christmas freeze in 1983—and another in 1985—killed almost every tree in the county. In the years since those one-two punches, Tavares and the area around it have bounced back. Citrus is no longer king, but a few growers have replanted and are actually producing small quantities of fruit.

Along with Eustis and Mount Dora, Tavares is part of a triangle of towns that have developed and prospered around some of the prettiest lakes in the state. This area is a haven for retirees, who continue to flock here. About 60 percent of Tavares consists of retirees. Previously, most headed north when the snow melted, but now, with air conditioning, many make this their permanent residence. Though they come from all parts of the northeast and Midwest, most of the Tavares retirees seem to be from Ohio and Michigan.

Even with the loss of the citrus trees, the scenery around Tavares is outstanding. Regardless of where you live in the town, it's only a short walk to either of the two lakes and a spectacular view, particularly at sunrise and sunset. Both are good sized bodies of water rimmed with many trees right down to the shoreline. It's a rare day you don't see many folks out in their boats, either fishing or just cruising around, enjoying the fresh air and the view.

Congregational church, Tavares, near the Dora Canal, once described as the "most beautiful mile of water in the world."

Tavares is a town noted for its preponderance of mobile and manufactured homes. Well over half of the town's residences are of this type. All of them, though, are not priced low. Some cost up to $100,000, and many others are close. Conventional homes also are available, and one developer is offering new two-bedroom, two-bath homes of conventional concrete block construction with many extras for $47,900. In an adult community just outside Tavares, one-story townhouse condos with two and three bedrooms and two baths start at $37,000.

The taxes here are reasonable, with a millage rate of only $3.85 in town and $12.51 in the county.

While Tavares is a very pleasant place to live, the town never quite achieved the greatness planned by its founder, Major Alexander St. Clair-Abrams. Naming the town in honor of one of his ancestors of noble birth, Abrams founded Tavares in 1880 with grandiose plans for its future. Tavares is a word of Portuguese origin meaning the hub. An attorney in Orlando, Abrams was a dynamic and irascible sort who envisioned Tavares as the capital of Florida. Even then peninsula residents were upset by the idea of the capital being stuck way up in the Panhandle at Tallahassee.

The Major built a sawmill and cigar factory to create jobs as his first move, then purchased the downtown section in 1880. Two years later he built the other half of Tavares and started constructing railroads to supply the town. By 1885 Tavares had been incorporated, but the dream of its becoming the capital had vanished. Instead, the Major and others began agitating to form a new county from parts of Orange and Sumter Counties. They succeeded, and Lake County was established the next year.

A bitter battle to settle on a county seat ensued over the next 13 months, with Tavares, Eustis and Leesburg all fighting for the courthouse. It took four elections, but Tavares finally emerged the winner.

Just when it appeared Tavares was on its way, a spark from a departing locomotive started a fire in April 1888 and nearly destroyed all of the business district. Then the historic freezes of 1894 and 1895 followed, forcing the railroads into receivership, wiping out the citrus and vegetable crops and killing every orange and grapefruit tree for miles around.

The next two decades were bleak indeed for Tavares. But the citrus growers eventually replanted and covered the countryside with fruit trees. Visitors from the north started discovering the scenic hills and lakes around here, and by the 1920s a full recovery had been achieved.

Recovery from the twin freezes of the 1980s was not as difficult for Tavares. By this time some industry had moved into town, and the retirees were continuing to migrate here in steadily increasing numbers. Many developers bought up the land where the citrus trees had been killed and started building homes, hundreds of them in every direction.

There are now four important industries in Tavares, the largest being Lake Regional Packing, a firm that employs 250 people in season and packs fresh fruit shipped into the area. Walker Stainless Steel Co., maker of steel containers, employs 75, and two trailer manufacturers, Fleetline and Space Masters, employ about another 200.

For residents of Tavares all the amenities are here. The town has a good recreation and parks system. Wooten Park, on Lake Dora, has lighted tennis courts, a children's playground, a boat ramp and a picnic shelter in a scenic setting. There are more picnic facilities at Summerall Park on the Dora Canal, and the town has plenty of recreational areas such as softball fields, a lighted baseball field and handball courts. Basketball and football facilities are planned, along with a renovated swimming pool. Six public golf courses are within ten miles of Tavares. In the middle of town is a large civic center that has a variety of uses. Behind the center are 16 shuffleboard courts.

Though the town has no hospital, it's only five miles to a major facility in neighboring Eustis. The city of Tavares provides excellent ambulance service to all hospitals in the area.

A library is centrally located and will be expanded soon to make room for a children's facility that has been occupying other quarters.

Tavares is fortunate in being centrally located, only an hour's drive from major attractions such as Disney World and

Sea World, and only five miles to the county's major shopping center, Lake Square Mall. The town has two shopping areas, older businesses along Main Street and ever new businesses cropping up on U.S. Highway 441 nearby. An old three-story brick building that dates from 1887 has been the city hall since 1979. A year after it was built, following the fire of 1888, it became a hotel with modern toilets and showers on every floor. Plans are afoot to restore it to its original look.

For educational needs, Lake Sumter Community College, only five miles away, offers adult education courses. Stetson, Rollins and the University of Central Florida are all within 40 miles from town.

The Lake County Historical Museum opened on Main Street in late 1988 with fine exhibits and tapes that give visitors a full description of what they're viewing.

The fire department, at the other end of Main Street, has taken over the brick depot formerly used by the Seaboard Coastline Railroad.

A community center houses all kinds of activities such as a Meals on Wheels program, a reading program for adults and youth, clogging lessons and community meetings. There's also a senior center in another building that serves hot meals at noon.

The biggest event of the year is Christmas by the Lake, held at Wooten Park over a two-day period in late November and featuring an arts and crafts show and food booths. A big July Fourth celebration also is held annually with fireworks.

Annexation in 1987 brought in over 600 new residents, but there are no big plans for further expansion. The only major project now under way is a waste water treatment plant being built at a cost of $5.2 million.

Back in the 20s, famous sportswriter Grantland Rice visited this area and took a ride through the Dora Canal, a mile-long connector between Lake Dora and Lake Eustis. He described it as "the most beautiful mile of water in the world."

The canal remains unchanged, and much of the area's other natural beauty has been preserved, despite all the growth. Both visitors and residents seem to agree that the area around this triangle of towns is among the most livable in Florida.

6. WEST CENTRAL

Brooksville

Population 7,500. West Central. North of Tampa, near gulf. Few permanent retirees. Large hospital, excellent library. Only incorporated town in county of 80,000. Hilly area. Main industry is limestone. Community college.

Until the 1970s, one of the more sparsely populated coastal areas of Florida was the west central counties north of Tampa on the Gulf of Mexico. One of these counties is Hernando, and its county seat is Brooksville.

From a meager population of 17,004 in 1970, Hernando had jumped to 80,000 by 1988 and is, according to Kiplinger, expected to hit 118,200 by 1997.

With all this population it is somewhat surprising to discover Brooksville is the only incorporated town in the county. The balance of the county is a hodgepodge of various developments, large and small, mobile home parks and tiny crossroad hamlets that are scattered about the landscape.

At 230 feet above sea level, Brooksville is one of the highest points on the gulf coast. The average elevation in the county is 175 feet, and this altitude, high for Florida, has been largely responsible for the mushrooming growth. Visitors to Florida started discovering this rolling countryside, the heavily forested areas of the county and the altitude which allows the cool breezes to flow into the county from the gulf.

Entering Brooksville from any direction, one sees it is a town built on hills. An old town, incorporated in 1880, it has impressive residential areas with several homes going back to the 19th century. The streets are lined with giant oak trees, and one of these, Brooksville Avenue, is one of the most scenic in Florida. The ancient oaks on this street have been allowed to form a canopy over the road with long strands of Spanish moss hanging in great profusion to make for a spectacular sight.

Brooksville is not a town that attracts many retirees on a permanent basis. There are 1,200 mobile homes in the town, but most of them are occupied only in the winter. Those folks head back to the northeast and Midwest when spring arrives and pay few taxes because of the Florida homestead exemption law.

In 1988 the population of Brooksville was estimated at 7,500, and there are no plans to annex new property unless the residents request it. Ambitious plans for improving the town don't include any major growth.

The biggest industry in Brooksville is limestone, used for road beds and in the manufacture of cement. The limestone mined in the area provides employment for 1,000 people. Trucks hauling this product fan out from the mines in all directions to various developments under construction up and down these fast growing gulf counties.

In addition to the limestone operations, Sparta Electronics makes sub-detector devices for the Defense Department and employs 350.

Agriculture is not a major industry in the area. Some peaches and tangerines were grown here until the 1970s, when a series of freezes killed them. They may come back later, but the replanting has been slow.

Many young people living in Brooksville commute to jobs in the Tampa Bay area. The unemployment rate is only 5.2 percent.

Another major factor in attracting new residents is the low cost of housing—well below the U.S. average with many three-bedroom, two-bath homes available in the $40,000 range. Apartments are fairly plentiful, and the rent for a one-bedroom is $350 per month.

Tax millage rates are about average for Florida, $8.2 in the city and between $15 and $16 in the county.

There are two major tourist attractions in the area, Rogers Christmas House in Brooksville and Weeki Wachee Springs, a few miles outside the town. The Christmas house started operations about 15 years ago and draws 250,000 visitors annually to shop through five old houses packed with gifts, ornaments and toys. Weeki Wachee attracts 500,000 a year and features a theater 16 feet underwater that presents live mermaid shows several times a day.

Recreational facilities are well balanced and include three parks. Two are city owned, one with three softball diamonds and another with an exercise trail, horseshoe pits and picnic grounds. A county-owned park downtown has four tennis courts, shuffleboard courts, a building for meetings, a children's playground and a bandshell.

There's a challenging private golf course in Brooksville, plus a public course and three semi-private courses elsewhere in the county. The public course is at Spring Hill, a development 15 miles away.

The scenic Withlacoochee River provides for most of the water sports. Several miles from town, it is good for canoeing and offers fishing from a bridge and limited swimming. The town has no swimming pool, and swimming on the gulf coast is limited to an area of about 100 yards because of the rough terrain.

One of the founding families of Brooksville was named Lykes, a stroke of good fortune for the town. The Lykes name is one of the biggest in Florida industry, the firm being a leader in meat packing as well as citrus.

Lykes Memorial Hospital in Brooksville has 166 beds and will be adding more. In the downtown area, one of the best small town libraries in the state opened in 1987 after major remodeling and enlarging. It's the Frederick Lykes Memorial Library, an outstanding structure with 60,000 volumes. The Lykes fortune supplied the funds for both buildings, as well as the Lykes Center for seniors, which opened in 1987.

Brooksville boasts of a long and somewhat colorful history. It started as Fort DeSoto in the 1840s and was named for Rep. Preston Brooks of South Carolina. During a Senate debate in 1856, Sen. Charles Sumner of Massachusetts denounced Sen.

A.P. Butler of South Carolina. Brooks resented the remarks, spotted Sumner in the Senate chamber and rapped him over the head with his cane, leaving him senseless on the floor. Folks around Hernando County heard about the attack, admired Brooks for his effort and named the county's largest settlement after him.

A recent addition to the local scene has been the Heritage Museum, a Victorian mansion with seven gables and 12 rooms built around 1850. It was obtained by a Brooksville historical association in 1981, and guided tours of the four-story structure are offered four days a week.

Education facilities in Brooksville are well above average. Approximately 54 percent of the high school graduates enroll in colleges and vocational schools. Pasco-Hernando Community College has a campus in town and serves 4,200 students, including many who take advantage of adult education courses.

Events staged each year are the Hernando County Fair, a classical music performance put on by the Brooksville Music Club at the Christmas season and the Brooksville Raid, held in January. The latter, drawing crowds of nearly 10,000, is a re-enactment of a Civil War battle fought in this area.

Business in Brooksville is centered around the courthouse square. The brick courthouse, built in 1912, has recently added a large annex for the new business being conducted there. Down the street from the courthouse, a new municipal building will replace the small city hall.

A 10-year plan calls for resurfacing the streets at a cost of $2.5 million. The city will preserve the original bricks that date back to 1878. A development group plans to rebuild three blocks of the downtown area. Meanwhile, an historical district is planned on Brooksville Avenue with the use of mostly private funds.

Brooksville will continue to be the financial center and service hub for the county. It's moving at a somewhat faster pace, but heavy traffic and the narrow streets will never permit any speeding. The small town atmosphere will always be there. It's quiet and reserved and still moving in the slow lane.

Cedar Key

Population 900. West Central. On island in Gulf of Mexico. Isolated fishing village. Nearest town 30 miles away. Few amenities, considerable history. Picturesque. Very quiet. Fishing is main activity. Attracts many tourists.

Any description of Cedar Key invariably includes the words unique and picturesque. This small town on an island in the Gulf of Mexico has those qualities in greater quantity than most any other place in Florida.

Battered by some of the worst hurricanes in the state's history, Cedar Key also has survived more than its share of economic woes through the years to remain alive and kicking. The tourists continue to flock here to admire the view and dine on some of the state's finest seafood.

Pollution-free waters allow seafood lovers to choose clams, oysters, shrimp, crab and fish from a typical gulf coast menu.

Where there once was a bustling community of 5,000, only 900 people now live in Cedar Key, on an island three miles from the mainland and connected to it by a series of small bridges. Between Chiefland, the nearest town 30 miles away, and Cedar Key there is nothing but thousands of acres of timber, marshland and a two-lane road—no houses, no people, plenty of small game and lots of birds. It's 45 miles to the nearest hospital in Williston, and the nearest city of any size is Gainesville, 60 miles away.

Essentially a fishing village, Cedar Key has many houses from the Victorian era, which help to give the town a distinct charm.

Life here is very quiet and peaceful, and the 900 who live here insist they would never want to live anywhere else. There's no nightlife, no fast-food restaurant, no movie theater. Everyone knows everyone else on a first name basis, and there's no apparent rush. If it doesn't get done today, there's always tomorrow.

A list of the town's amenities is quite short. There are no cultural activities, though several artists and writers live here on a year-round basis. The only recreational facilities, except for a small swimming beach at the city park downtown, are at the Cedar Key school. A small library is open four days a week and is going into newly constructed quarters behind the city hall. No senior services are offered, aside from a bus that takes the seniors to Chiefland every Friday for shopping, doctors appointments or any other errands.

For those needing hospitalization, the town is well prepared. Cedar Key has an ambulance service, and an air ambulance service can whisk patients by helicopter to one of four major hospitals in Gainesville in minutes.

Living costs in Cedar Key probably are higher than in most towns, largely because of the isolation. There's only a single grocery in town, one hardware, a newspaper and three banks. Most of the other businesses in town, including nine restaurants, a dozen hotels and motels, three RV parks and three seafood stores, cater primarily to the tourists. Real estate prices are higher than most small towns, and there's very little home construction. Only three building permits were issued in 1988. Because of its somewhat precarious location in the gulf, residents are environmentally conscious, and there is no pollution of any consequence in the waters around Cedar Key. Growth is well managed through very tough zoning regulations. Though there are so few people here, the zoning code, adopted in 1984, extends over 300 pages. The town is without any traffic light as a result of the zoning code, which devotes 15 pages to this subject.

Drinking water for Cedar Key comes from deep wells on the mainland, six miles away. An electric co-op provides power. The town's businesses are largely confined to a single street. All of the buildings are old and most are weather-beaten from long exposure to the relentless Florida sun and the winds off the gulf.

On this street is the Island Hotel, a Cedar Key fixture that's been in continuous operation since 1846. On the National Register of Historic Places, it once housed Confederate and Union troops at different times and was a favorite writing retreat for Pearl Buck. There's a pot bellied stove in the lobby, a tiny bar, a dining room that serves excellent seafood and ten rooms. Little has been changed since 1846.

There are two museums in town, one in the business section that's locally operated, and another that the state runs on the outskirts. Both are well stocked and provide a thorough look at the intriguing history of Cedar Key.

There is archaeological evidence of Indians having lived on Cedar Key as early as 500 A.D. While Cedar Key wasn't settled until the early 1840s, it's packed a wealth of history into the comparatively short period since then. Few Florida towns can match it in that department. The town didn't really flourish until the state's first cross-Florida railroad was built between Fernandina on the east coast and Cedar Key. David Levy Yulee, for whom Levy County was named, was responsible for the railroad, which was completed in 1861. There were about 80 to 100 people living on the Cedar Keys then. This railroad allowed shipment of lumber, turpentine and other products, and Cedar Key became a booming port city. The town was incorporated in 1867.

Indian wars also played a major role in Cedar Key's history.

The big island of Atsena Otie, a half mile south of the Cedar Key dock area, was used as a military depot and staging area. When the wars ended, a man named Augustus Steele, called the Father of Cedar Key, bought the island and its military buildings for $227. The island then became the nucleus for the first white settlement in the area.

After the railroad arrived, thousands of acres of cedar trees in the area were cut down. In the late 1860s, 17 sawmills in Cedar Key were turning out a half million feet of lumber every week. Much of the wood was used in the manufacture of pencils with large plants on both Atsena Otie Key and Cedar Key. This had become the largest producing area of pencils in the U.S., and the population had zoomed to 5,000 by 1887.

In 1884 Henry Plant built a rival railroad connecting Tampa to the east coast. This signaled the beginning of the end for Cedar Key's boom. In 1882 over 300 steamships had put in at the port of Cedar Key, but four years later only 30 ships arrived. Local residents turned to the sea for a living, and about a million pounds of seafood were shipped out each year.

The final blow for Cedar Key came in 1896 when a tidal surge from a hurricane swept a 10-foot wall of water onto the islands. Atsena Otie Key was abandoned forever, the pencil plants badly damaged and several lumber mills destroyed by the wind and storm surge. Two local hotels burned down, and the railroad connecting Cedar Key to the mainland was washed away. Forestry operations were finished.

As the 20th century started, Cedar Key had become a "has been." Less than 50 people voted in the 1900 election. Another blow hit in 1909 when the black point oyster had become overharvested and was closed to commercial fishing for 30 years. Amidst all these misfortunes, Cedar Key hung on and started a fiber factory that manufactured brooms and brushes from palmetto palms. The plant had 100 employees and operated from 1910 to 1950.

By 1950, synthetic fibers and cheaper imports were threatening the Cedar Key plant. Then another monstrous hurricane hit. The winds reached such velocity that the machine recording them blew away. Estimates ranged from 135 to 185 miles per hour. Ninety-five percent of the buildings in Cedar Key were damaged, and the fiber plant was out of business.

There have been other hurricanes since, but none to match those giants of 1896 and 1950. Hurricane Elena hit in 1985, but its winds were only about 80 miles per hour. Part of the highway into town was washed away, and the water lines were broken. Residents had to use portable toilets and rely on drinking water being trucked into town for about three weeks.

Some might feel Cedar Key is almost like a punch-drunk fighter that doesn't know when he's had enough. One less than generous writer described the place as "a dowager with missing teeth." Despite all the hurricanes, the economic misfortunes and its isolation from the rest of the civilized world, Cedar Key seems to hang in there. The people who live here and aren't natives say they fell in love with it at first sight. The natives wouldn't even consider leaving, and the tourists love it and keep coming back.

A professor at the University of Central Florida, over 150 miles away in Orlando, owns a home in Cedar Key and flies back and forth each weekend with his wife. A lawyer, also from Orlando, drives here each weekend while his wife stays in their home in Cedar Key on a full-time basis.

There are three special events staged each year. The biggest of these is a seafood festival in November. This includes an arts and crafts show, a boat show, a parade and beauty contest. Held annually since 1970, it draws 30,000 to 40,000 and offers lots of booths serving seafood and other dishes. A big July 4th celebration has a parade, fireworks over the gulf and activities in the city park. The emphasis here is not so much on seafood but hot dogs and lemonade. In April there's an art festival that has extensive displays of art in a juried show. Food booths are again set up for this event.

There's no industry on the island, so most residents make their living from commercial fishing or service jobs. Quite a few retirees have settled here, many of them attracted by the unlimited fishing opportunities. There's a big fishing pier on the dock with benches up and down both sides. Fish caught here include redfish, Spanish mackerel, whiting, flounder and speckled trout. Many do their fishing from boats and catch pompano and grouper in the deeper water. Mullet is one of the most common fish in the area. Oysters are plentiful except during the summer months, while blue crabs and stone crabs are always in good supply. Launching and docking facilities for boats are available. A few miles north of Cedar Key is the mouth of the Suwannee River, a good spot for digging clams.

Within five miles of Cedar Key is the Cedar Keys Wildlife Refuge, comprised of several off-shore islands that range from six to 165 acres in size. Established by Herbert Hoover in 1929, the islands provide ideal nesting and feeding conditions for the brown pelican. More than 1,200 of this endangered species have been recorded on Seahorse Key, where a lighthouse built in 1855 is still standing. All of the keys are a bird watcher's paradise.

Prices for real estate vary greatly, depending on the location. A three-bedroom, two-bath home away from the water will cost about $95,000. On the water these homes run from $150,000 to $200,000. Lots on the water can be as low as $25,000 and as high as $130,000. Some lots are $85,000 on the water and just $35,000 across the street. Rentals are scarce in winter and run about $750 a month for an apartment or small cottage. The tax millage rate is $5.5.

In the downtown area, the only construction going on recently has been renovation of the city hall. It was formerly the private home of the lady now serving as town clerk, so she is conducting the town's business from what had been her bedroom.

There are no plans for spectacular growth. The town's population has increased from 700 in the 1980 census to its present 900, and there's no agitation for accommodating many more residents. Those who do migrate here and settle are likely to stick around for a long time. At least that's been the usual pattern around Cedar Key. There's no other place quite like it in Florida and none likely to pop up anytime in the future.

Crystal River

Population 3,778. West Central. 75 miles north of Tampa, near gulf. Heavy growth in nearby areas. Fishing, boating, swimming popular. New library, good hospital. State museum. Many retirees in area.

As recently as the 1920s there were only 69 telephones in the town of Crystal River, and cattle still roamed the streets. In the six decades since, this scenic spot near the Gulf of Mexico has become a mecca for water enthusiasts from all parts of Florida and a growing area for retirees.

Located about 75 miles north of Tampa in an area where the gulf coast starts to bend west along Florida's Panhandle, Crystal River is another of those places that was slow to develop.

There were only 927 people living here in 1940 and 1,026 in 1950. Now the figure is 3,778, and another 8,000 plus are living in the immediate surrounding areas. Crystal River is one of only two incorporated towns in Citrus County, which has zoomed from just 9,268 population in 1960 to an estimated 88,000. The other incorporated town is Inverness, the county seat, but that's inland, and most of the growth has been closer to the gulf.

Water has been the major attraction in Crystal River, and there is never a shortage. The town acquired its name from the Crystal River, which originates at large underground springs and flows seven miles to the gulf. Even with all the civilization in the area, the stream still is crystal clear and available for a wide variety of activities. Just south of Crystal River are two more streams which also originate from springs, the Homosassa and the Chassahowitzka.

Most folks who live in the area spend considerable time relaxing on or near these rivers or the gulf. There's excellent fishing of both the fresh and salt water variety, plus plenty of space for boating, swimming, scuba diving and snorkeling. For those who prefer a quieter spot, the Withlacoochee River, one of the state's most scenic streams flows north and forms the eastern and northern boundaries of Citrus County.

The town of Crystal River is not on the gulf, but any kind of boat will get you there in a hurry. Despite all the housing developments going up around the area and the great influx of people, there is still plenty of open space. There are many good hunting areas, and camping is popular with both residents and visitors. Crystal River is definitely a tourist town.

Kings Bay is the large body of water that Crystal River has been built around, and the freshwater springs in the bay are the second largest in the state. These springs pour out over two million gallons of crystal clear water every minute, and the temperature is always the same, 72 degrees.

With all this clear water, it's not surprising that scuba divers from all over the U.S. gather at Kings Bay to explore the springs off Banana Island and observe the manatees. These acquatic mammals number between 60 and 100 and arrive in November to escape the colder waters in the gulf. Visible from boats, these gentle creatures weigh from 1,000 to 2,000 pounds. Divers and snorkelers are often approached by the manatees, who want to have their backs and stomachs scratched.

Fishing is a major sport and business here. For those preferring fresh water, the most common varieties are speckled perch, bluegill, shellcrackers and catfish. In the salt water, the anglers try their luck on silver and speckled trout, grouper, Spanish mackerel, redfish, pompano, cobia, shark and ladyfish. Fishing guides are available for both types. In addition to the fishing, there's also scalloping, shrimping, oystering and crabbing going on daily in the gulf. Marked channels in Crystal River lead to the gulf.

With so many fish around, it's not surprising that there are several local restaurants that feature seafood on the menu and offer patrons spectacular views of the many rivers, lakes and bays of the area.

The area has a long and colorful history. Prior to the arrival of the early settlers, this area along the gulf coast was inhabited by Timucuan Indians from about 200 B.C. to 1400 A.D. Hernando De Soto hiked through Citrus County in 1539 and traded with the Seminole Indians who lived in the woods and coves of the Withlacoochee.

The Timucuans left behind considerable evidence of their culture, enough to stock the Crystal River State Museum just outside the town. It's the site of a pre-historic Indian settlement, and it's open Thursday through Sunday. The Indians lived on an abundant supply of shellfish, casting away the empty shells which formed the large Indian mounds near the museum. More than 450 burials have been discovered there since 1903, and the Indians' ceremonial mounds still exist.

In 1842 the federal government offered 160 acres of free land to anyone who worked at least five acres, had a gun and ammunition, built a house and defended it from the Seminole Indians. By the following year the Indians had been shipped to the Everglades, and by 1844 the area had been surveyed and settlers were starting to arrive.

By the mid 1850s the first post office had been established, and the population had climbed to 100 in 1880. It doubled in the next five years.

In those early years, there were great stands of cedar trees in the area, and a cedar mill was founded in 1884 to produce pencils, cedar lining for closets and cedar oil for soaps and perfumes.

In Crystal River, the largest employer is Florida Power Corp., which built a nuclear plant in the area and has 1,000 employees. There are several boat builders in town, and the modern Seven Rivers Community Hospital, a facility with 112 beds and a staff of 50 specialists, employs another 200.

The town has made important gains in recent years. Retirees account for about 25 percent of the population in Crystal River, and there are thousands more in the various developments springing up around the town.

Because this is the only town of much size in this area on the gulf, there has been heavy commercial development in Crystal River. A large shopping center opened in 1988, and the Edward J. DeBartolo Corp. is planning a large shopping mall on Highway 19 that will include four department stores. Also planned is an 800 unit housing project. This is in addition to the Crystal River Village and its 540 units just outside the city limits, which will be finished by 1995.

Not all of the retirees and new residents are from states to the north. Many from other parts of Florida, particularly the larger cities, have found the easy life-style of Crystal River more to their liking.

The town has much to offer beside all the activity on the water. There are ten golf courses in the county, two of them in the immediate area. Centennial Field has lighted tennis courts, racquetball courts and baseball and softball fields.

For the swimmers, there's the Fort Island Gulf Beach, complete with showers and parking, and another nice beach at Hunter Springs Park, closer to town.

Cultural activities haven't been neglected. An active Citrus Actors Theater puts on four productions each year, and the Citrus County Art League sponsors several art festivals, shows and classes. The major event of the year is the Manatee Festival, lasting nearly two weeks in November and including an arts and crafts show, seafood festival, beauty pageant, canoe race and antique show.

A new town library opened in 1987 is stocked with nearly 30,000 volumes.

Crystal River, known for its outstanding recreational opportunities, maintains a laid-back life-style. (New library, above).

A wide variety of homes at reasonable prices is available in Crystal River, including single homes of all sizes, condos and well maintained mobile home parks and manufactured homes. The tax millage rate is $5.26.

Laid-back is the only way to describe the life-style in Crystal River. The area continues to grow and prosper as more and more people discover this area of Florida, but there are no plans for the town becoming a major population center. Projections for the population by the next century put the total at only 5,841 in 2010. And that seems to suit the residents just fine.

Dade City

Population 5,500. West Central. 40 miles northeast of Tampa. Few retirees. Citrus still big, despite freeze. Major packing plant. Steep hills in area. Fishing, canoeing nearby. Large hospital. Community college.

Steep hills are not common on the Florida peninsula, so a trip to Dade City gives some the impression they are in another state. Many of the roads leading into the town are almost like roller coasters and the views from atop these big hills are impressive.

Unlike most other towns on the peninsula, Dade City is not a haven for retirees. There are a few who have migrated here from up north, but they constitute a small percentage of the population of 5,500.

This is an area dedicated primarily to agriculture. Tourists aren't discouraged from visiting, but Dade City is not a tourist oriented town. In the rolling countryside surrounding the town, the main agricultural interests are citrus, cattle and poultry. The citrus people got caught by the same Christmas freeze of '83 that struck so many areas of Florida, but they aren't quitting here. Over 60 percent of the orange and grapefruit trees have been replanted.

Citrus still provides a major source of income for Dade City residents. The huge Lykes-Pasco Packing Co. plant here em-

125

ploys 1,400 during the peak of the season and about 800 during the off-season. Since the freeze much of the fruit for processing has to be shipped in from areas south of Dade City that weren't affected.

In 1987 Dade City was selected for the Florida Main Street Program and is busy with plans to spruce up its downtown sector. Many of the older businesses and the county government buildings are located there, while the supermarkets and chains are on a major highway on the edge of town.

The town has very attractive residential sections, quiet and shady streets with a mix of new and older homes that are well maintained. It strikes one immediately as a good town for raising a family, and the residents seem to agree. They tell you the life-style is quiet and safe with very little crime. Quite a few local people commute to jobs in Tampa, 30 minutes away.

In addition to the Lykes plant, county government and health care account for much of the employment. Dade City is the county seat of Pasco County, and a large new courthouse was added in 1980 to augment the little domed courthouse built back in 1909. This county, 16th fastest growing in the U.S., has a population of over 250,000, so the courthouse conducts considerable business.

Humana Hospital, a very modern facility, has 120 beds and a staff of over 70 physicians. Other industries in town are manufacturers of septic tanks and concrete pipe.

Real estate prices here are quite reasonable, the median price for homes running between $60,000 and $65,000. The millage rate is $5.40 in the city and $21.77 in the county.

Unlike the western part of the county, where retirees have been flocking in large numbers for the last 15 years or more, Dade City has not experienced any spectacular growth. From a population of only 36,785 in 1960, Pasco has jumped to more than a quarter million now. Dade City, meanwhile, was 4,759 in 1960, and nearly 30 years later, it's only about 5,500. There are nearly 30,000 more in the surrounding area, but they are well spread out.

People living around Dade City contend that the lack of overcrowding is what they most like about the place. Plenty of wide open spaces remain, and the area is still scenic, despite the loss of so many citrus groves. The town is a short distance from the Withlacoochee River, where fishing and canoeing are popular sports. There are dozens of lakes in the immediate area, many of which have public boat ramps. Lake Pasadena is another popular fishing area. There's enough wilderness around the Withlacoochee and other sections to take care of large populations of deer, bobcats and alligators. In the spring the wilderness areas become a giant bird sanctuary for many wading birds, blue and white herons and American wood storks.

The town has an interesting history and is one of central Florida's oldest incorporated places, celebrating the centennial of its incorporation in 1987. Major Francis Dade of the U.S. Infantry is the man the town was named after. Having camped in the area during an ill-fated march from Tampa to Ocala in 1835, he was later massacred by Seminole Indians in December of that year.

Even without many retirees here, there still are the usual shuffleboard courts, and they're lighted. Other recreational facilities include lighted tennis courts and several softball and baseball fields. There's a civic center located near the courthouse that serves as a focal point for many of the town's clubs and their activities. It has a portable stage and also is used for the summer recreation program.

In town there's an 18-hole golf course at the Town and Country Club, while a very scenic course is only five miles away at the little town of St. Leo. The latter is a public course and may be the hilliest course in the state.

Swimmers have their choice of a public beach at Clear Lake outside the city or an Olympic sized pool at St. Leo.

St. Leo is the site of a four-year college with an enrollment of 1,100, which will celebrate its centennial in 1989. In Dade City there's an attractive campus of Pasco Hernando Community College, one of three such campuses in the two counties. It offers a wide range of subjects, and adult education courses also are available. The high school, with the somewhat unusual name of Pasco Comprehensive High School, is on a hilly campus at the edge of town.

A new library, opened in 1963, has already outgrown its space, and will be doubled in size. There are 20,000 volumes, and more will be added with the new quarters. A busy Heritage Arts Association puts on five dramatic performances each year at the various schools in the area. There's a private art gallery in town, and St. Leo and Pasco Hernando Community College both host fine arts series on an annual basis. Open since 1961, Florida Pioneer Museum is one of Florida's more interesting preservations of the state's history and certainly worth a visit. It started with a variety of old farm equipment, which is housed along with other memorabilia in the main museum. To that has been added a restored house that was built in 1864, a one-room schoolhouse from another town and an old railroad depot, complete with a steam engine. Spread over a wooded 16 acres, it's open every day but Monday. City planners are anticipating some of the county's growth to expand to Dade City during the next decade. It is estimated that 20,000 people now work or shop there. Annexation is difficult because of state statutes, but they still expect an addition of 10,000 population by the turn of the century. Some of these may petition to be annexed.

Until all that growth happens, Dade City will continue to enjoy life as something of an island of tranquility amidst a county growing in proportions nobody would have dreamed possible just 20 years ago.

Dunnellon

Population 2,000. West Central. 25 miles southwest of Ocala. Many retirees. Quiet life-style. At junction of two scenic rivers, good fishing. New high school. Two large developments north of town. Small growth expected.

It's just a quiet and peaceful little town now on the banks of two very scenic rivers, but in its earlier days Dunnellon was one of the roughest spots in Florida. Today fishing and tourism are the biggest businesses in town. Nearly a century ago, Dunnellon was the center of the phosphate mining industry in Florida and a typically rowdy boomtown.

A farmer drilling for a well discovered phosphate by accident in 1889, and the boom followed, lasting for over 20 years. The decline started during World War I when the phosphate couldn't be shipped to the usual markets in Europe. Then phosphate was discovered in Hillsborough and Polk Counties and by the mid-1920s the industry had closed its Dunnellon operations entirely.

It's difficult to imagine Dunnellon as a boomtown with all the accompanying lawlessness. The town acquired lights and a water system during that boisterous era because each of the town's 13 saloons paid taxes of $1,000. Now it's so quiet here the loudest noise of the day may be the bass or other fish breaking the surface of the Withlacoochee or Rainbow Rivers.

There are about 2,000 people living in Dunnellon and about the same number at the big Rainbow Springs development just north of town. The life-style is definitely laid-back.

Begun in the 1840s, the early settlement became a refuge for fugitive slaves and deserters from both the Union and Confederate armies during the Civil War.

By 1887 the town was platted, and incorporation followed in 1891. The town was named after John F. Dunn, the founder and early promoter of Dunnellon. How the 'ellon' part of the name was acquired is still something of a mystery. Some early historians reported Dunn's wife was named Ellen, and that accounted for the latter part of the town's name. Later research revealed his wife's name was Alice, so the 'ellon' part is still unexplained.

There were 700 residents here at the turn of the century, but this figure had jumped to 1,300 by the time the city hall was built in 1910. With the phosphate boom over, Dunnellon stood still and had only 1,344 residents by 1945. The banks closed during the depression in 1931, and there was no bank in town again until 1946.

In the years since the end of World War II, Dunnellon has become a favorite with retirees and a haven for both hunters and fishermen. The Withlacoochee and Rainbow Rivers meet in Dunnellon, and the point of that meeting is where many of the larger bass are caught.

About seven miles north of Dunnellon is Rainbow Springs, the headwaters of the Rainbow River. The springs produce nearly 500 million gallons of clear, sparkling water every day. A tourist attraction flourished in the 60s and early 70s at Rainbow Springs but closed in 1973 and is used now as a park by Rainbow Springs residents.

Nearly 700 homes have been built at Rainbow Springs, and most of the residents are retirees. The homes are impressive, and there is a variety of floor plans. Prices range from $98,500 for 1,813 square feet of living space to $118,500 for 2,444 square feet. The development includes a scenic 18-hole golf course.

Also in the same general area is an even larger development, Rainbow Lake Estates. Started in 1960, this complex now has 1,200 homes and about 2,800 residents. Spread over 13,000 acres, it is expected to become home to nearly 30,000 people by the time of its completion.

In Dunnellon there are several nice residential districts, and one of the best lies along the heavily shaded banks of the Withlacoochee. Funds for roads and schools are provided by the county government out of property tax money paid by residents of the developments.

Homes with three bedrooms and two baths are priced under $50,000, and several with two bedrooms and two baths are in the $35,000 range. These reasonable prices attract the retirees. The town millage rate is $6.06. There's also a mobile home village in Dunnellon, but no single mobile homes are allowed in the town.

Shopping facilities in town have increased substantially in recent years with the addition of two large shopping centers at the north end of the business district, along U.S. Highway 41. For those interested in more extensive shopping there are larger stores and malls in Crystal River and Ocala. The latter is 24 miles from Dunnellon and is the largest city in the area.

There's no industry in town, but unemployment is not a problem. Many residents commute to jobs in Ocala, and the various construction projects in the area provide employment on a year-round basis for quite a few more.

Most of the fishing in Dunnellon is from boats in the two rivers. Rules are strict on the Rainbow, a fragile stream, and no open containers are permitted in the boats. In addition to bass, there is a large variety of panfish available. Fishing lodges and camps abound in the area. The Withlacoochee empties into the Gulf of Mexico only about 20 miles west of Dunnellon, so fishermen seeking salt water can be there in a short time.

Wild game in the unpopulated areas near Dunnellon make this a hunter's paradise. There are deer, wild hog, turkey and quail in large numbers nearby and in the Ocala National Forest farther east.

Recreational facilities in Dunnellon are very limited. Most of these are at the new high school east of town. There is swimming at the beach where the two rivers meet, and there are two 18-hole golf courses and one 9-hole course in the area. A Little League field is on the edge of town.

Though Dunnellon has no hospital, there are two large ones in Ocala and a new hospital 20 miles away in Crystal River.

There's a very adequate library that's open six days a week and has over 10,000 volumes. The nearest college, Central Florida Community College in Ocala, offers adult education courses, as does a high school in Lecanto, a few miles south of Dunnellon. Art and drama enthusiasts get involved in active groups in neighboring Citrus County at the towns of Crystal River and Inverness.

As in most towns of this size that are not close to any large cities, much of the activity centers around the schools. An ultra-modern high school was built in the late 80s and is used extensively by the residents of Dunnellon. One long-time resident says the building of this new high school was the best thing that's happened to Dunnellon in the last 50 years. He feels it did wonders for local morale. Previously the high school students were squeezed into an old building in town and overflowed into temporary classrooms.

The town has come a long way in the approximately 50 years since gambling was outlawed by the legislature. It had been legal before 1936, and most businesses in Dunnellon had slot machines in the stores or lined up in front of the stores. Now the only betting around here is over who will catch the day's largest fish from the two rivers.

In April, the town remembers its past and stages a Boomtown Festival. It takes place on the third weekend of the month and includes an arts and crafts show, blue-grass music, food booths, contests for the kids and a beauty pageant. The folks dress up in the costumes of that lusty era, and the stores try to emulate the same period.

In April 1990 the town's centennial will be celebrated, and it will last until April 1991. By that time the Dunnellon city limits may have been expanded. The town fathers are hopeful of some annexation to increase their tax base. Even without it, the town seems confident of prospering. It's located in an idyllic setting and continues to lure many folks who are looking for a quiet and friendly town in which to raise their families or relax and enjoy their retirement.

Inverness

Population 5,000. West Central. 70 miles north of Tampa, near gulf. Many retirees. Large hospital, new library. Adult education center. On large lake. Good recreational, cultural facilities. British owned hotel.

Among any list of Florida's prettiest towns, Inverness would have few challengers. Its natural beauty places it near the top of the list.

Approaching this Citrus County town from the east, the view is magnificent. After crossing the Withlacoochee River, one of the state's most scenic streams, it's a drive along miles of water on both sides of the highway, going by Lake Tsala Apopka and continuing right to the city limits of Inverness. In any description of Inverness, this waterfront would have to be considered the most dramatic feature of the town.

Lake Tsala Apopka is actually a chain of lakes and marshes that extends north and south of Inverness for several miles. A drive along this chain is 22 miles long and covers 24,000

On Lake Tsala Apopka, Inverness, one of Florida's prettiest towns, boasts an excellent school system. (Above, courthouse).

acres. From the air the town appears to be an island set amidst all this water.

With so much water at its doorstep, it's not surprising that water sports play a big part in the community's life-style. Indeed, Tsala Apopka is an Indian phrase for "trout eating place." This chain of lakes, plus 45 miles of riverfront on the Withlacoochee, provides plenty of space for boating, sailing, water skiing, fishing and scuba diving. On the Withlacoochee canoeing is very popular as the participants paddle their way up and down those 45 miles in the county and even beyond. Civilization seems hundreds of miles away in this idyllic setting. Only the birds break the silence as the boaters drift through virgin forests, now and then casting a line or just leaning back and absorbing the tranquility and scenery.

Inverness has been a town since 1887 and is the seat of Citrus County, one of those west central Florida counties on the Gulf of Mexico experiencing skyrocketing growth in the 1970s and 1980s. The county had only 9,268 residents in 1960 but had leaped to 88,000 by 1988 and is projected to be over 105,000 by 2000.

Despite this growth, much of which has occurred in the western part of the county and the gulf, Inverness has not experienced any huge increase. The population is only a little above 5,000, though the Inverness post office serves 14,000 homes, indicating a fairly heavy development in the surrounding area.

After driving along the spectacular waterfront of Lake Tsala Apopka and into the main business district of Inverness, visitors get a start as they suddenly find a three-story hotel that appears to have been transplanted from England. This is the Crown Hotel, and it's a rare jewel, boasting leaded glass doors, a crystal chandelier and hand-rubbed spiral staircase. There are 31 rooms in this British-owned inn priced unbelievably low, $45 per night for a single and $57 for a double.

Built as a general store over 90 years ago, a British group discovered what was then the run-down Orange Hotel in 1979 and spent 18 months plus $2 million restoring it to the splendor of the Victorian era. An antique double-decker bus is parked near the canopied entry. Inside, the guests have their choice of rooms with brass headboards, tufted velvet chairs, tasselled draperies and coordinated bath with gold-plated fixtures. Downstairs is Churchill's Restaurant, offering outstanding dining and service.

The Inverness business district fans out from the old courthouse on the square near Lake Tsala Apopka. This courthouse was built in 1912, and when the population boom hit, a new courthouse was built next to it in 1977.

Agriculture is not a major industry in Citrus County. Despite the name, the county has only about 150 acres of citrus. There had been an orange boom back in the 1880s, but a major freeze in 1895 wiped out citrus, and the area never was a large grower again. Phosphate also experienced a boom in the first decade of the 20th century, but later declined sharply and is only a small operation now. Floral City, a little town near Inverness, is only 1,100 population now but had 10,000 residents during the height of the phosphate boom. In 1885, when its population was 300, Floral City was twice the size of Miami.

Among Florida's 67 counties, Citrus County rates 57th in agricultural production. But, as one long-time real estate salesman points out, "We have found that this land is much more profitable when it's used for planting Yankees." There can be no quarrel with this statement, as the retirees continue to pour into Inverness and the surrounding area in search of homes and property. A third of the population is retirees, many of whom came from the more populous areas of Florida. They're impressed with the scenery, the easy paced life and the cultural opportunities that make this such a desirable area.

Recreation is important around here, and much of it is concentrated in a single spot, Whispering Pines Park, one of the largest city-owned and operated parks in the state. Located in a wooded setting on the edge of town, it offers four lighted tennis courts, six lighted shuffleboard courts, five lighted racquetball courts, a lighted junior Olympic sized swimming pool, a 2.5 mile jogging, biking and nature trail, three baseball fields and sheltered picnic area with fireplace, grills and a playground area for the kids. There is no admission fee. Just south of Inverness is Fort Cooper State Park, which has a beautiful sand-bottom lake for swimming.

There are 10 public golf courses in the area, and three of them are in Inverness. Many golf tournaments are held in the county each year.

Living costs in Inverness are not high. The most popular homes are priced from $50,000 to $60,000. Condos are not selling well, so the developers are continuing to build houses. The millage rate is $21.07 in Inverness and $12.77 in the county.

As an indication of how great the building boom has been in Citrus County in the 1980s, 14,391 homes were built from April 1980 to April 1986, an average of 200 per month for six years.

Education is at a high level around here. The county scored ahead of the national average in every grade level and in all subjects tested in the McGraw Hill comprehensive test of basic skills.

A branch of Central Florida Community College is located in Lecanto, six miles away, while a large vocational and adult education center is in Inverness. The latter offers a lengthy list of courses that includes such diverse subjects as carpentry, nursing, electrical wiring, sign language, Spanish, German, bead stringing, guitar and oil painting. The center can accommodate 2,000 students in night classes.

A recent addition to the Inverness scene is the Lakes Region Library, opened in 1987. It's a well-planned building with 20,000 volumes and is open six days a week.

Another valuable Inverness asset is Citrus Memorial Hospital, built in 1956 with 160 beds.

In the field of culture, Inverness is a busy place. The Citrus County Art League has its own building and stages a major art show each November. A Citrus Actors Theater group is active and puts on five productions each year. A county museum is on the first floor of the old county courthouse. This includes an Indian Exhibit Hall that opened in 1985 and was researched, designed and built by the Withlacoochee River Archeology Council.

It's been a long time since Juan Ponce de Leon was the first Spaniard to visit Citrus County. In the years since, the procession of visitors has drastically increased. So far, Inverness and the surrounding area seem to be able to cope with this invasion.

Zephyrhills

Population 7,000. West Central. 35 miles northeast of Tampa. Noted for good drinking water. Many mobile home parks outside town. Third of population retired. Senior center, hospital, library. Center for parachuting.

While it may be near the bottom of the list in any alphabetical roll call, Zephyrhills is well ahead in at least two categories. This west central Florida town is the home of some of the best drinking water in the state, and in numbers of mobile home parks, the Zephyrhills area may well be the capital of Florida.

Within the city limits of Zephyrhills there is only a handful of mobile home parks, which is about average for most Florida towns. In the surrounding area, though, they are scattered over the landscape in great profusion. By the summer of 1988 the number of these parks had skyrocketed to over 150, which means thousands of mobile homes. Some are quite impressive and can cost over $50,000. Most, though, are fairly small, are used only during the winter months and are packed together like soldiers in a close-order drill.

Zephyrhills' permanent population is about 7,000, but the surrounding area has another 20,000 on a year-round basis. In the winter the number of area residents jumps to approximately 75,000. And still more mobile home parks are planned outside the city. In Zephyrhills about a third of the population is retired, and most of these are from New York and Michigan. The mobile homes outside the city are occupied almost exclusively by retirees. When the snow melts up north, they're on their way back home.

While the residents of Zephyrhills don't discourage these mobile home people, this great concentration of them is not listed among the town's leading assets. The number one claim to fame is the drinking water, pure crystal water that comes from seven of the deepest wells in Florida. Stored in tanks, this great tasting water is sold by the city to a commercial firm which bottles and peddles it in trucks all over the state. With the threat of salt-water intrusion of Florida's ground water and the constant fear of pollution, sales of this Zephyrhills water escalate each year. It's a major business.

In addition to the water distributors the largest employers are Zephyr Egg, which employs 150 people, and Lykes-Pasco, a juice dispensing firm which has 72 employees. There's also an electronics assembly plant in town.

Many local residents, mostly in the 23 to 35 age bracket, commute to jobs in the Tampa area, an hour's drive away.

Zephyrhills refers to itself as "The Friendly City of Pure Water," and is a town which takes justifiable pride in its residential districts. Located on tree-lined, well lighted streets, a great majority of the homes are well above average. Even in the intense heat of summer, these shady streets and parks make life outside quite bearable.

The area was hard hit by the great freezes of 1983 and 1985, which affected so many other citrus-growing areas in this same latitude, but the owners of many of the dead orange trees came up with a ready solution. They bulldozed out the dead trees and started building parks for mobile homes. Most all mobile home parks have been built in the last 15 years, and a majority since the twin freezes. Not all the growers, though, turned to mobile home parks for their salvation. Some are replanting and betting against any more killer freezes.

Living costs are not high in Zephyrhills. The tax millage rate is $6.8 in the city and $14.5 in the county. Real estate prices are not unreasonable, and good 3-bedroom homes may be purchased in the $50,000 range. Rentals are available, but they're tight in the winter.

Zephyrhills is in Pasco County, which has been one of Florida's fastest growing counties in recent years. Its population has zoomed from about 36,000 in 1960 to more than 250,000 in the late 1980s. Fortunately for the Zephyrhills area most of this growth has occurred in the western part of the county, nearer the Gulf of Mexico. The eastern portion is still largely rural.

The town doesn't have a long history. In the early 1900s the land here was covered with virgin pines. The trees were tapped for turpentine, then cut for lumber, the stumps uprooted and pushed out. Then the land was seeded to pasture or set in citrus groves.

By 1909, the site was chosen for a veterans colony by Capt. H.B. Jeffries, a Civil War veteran, because of the elevation, the fertile land and abundance of good water. Also, there were no swamps in the area, and that meant no malaria or mosquitoes.

While Jeffries was showing the countryside to some prospective residents one day, he overhead a remark about the rolling hills and zephyr-like breezes, and in 1910 Zephyrhills became the name of what had been called Abbott Station. The town was incorporated in 1914.

There were only 1,826 people here in 1950, so the population has more than tripled in less than 40 years. With that growth Zephyrhills has managed to keep pace by adding the amenities that make this one of the area's more desirable places to live.

The recreational needs have not been neglected. There are nine tennis courts with five of them lighted for night play, four golf courses in the immediate area, numerous softball and baseball fields, racquetball courts, hiking trails and exercise trails. An active Tourist Club in the downtown area has lighted shuffleboard courts. For the swimmers there's a small beach at the Recreation Center plus nearby Crystal Springs Recreational Preserve. A new swimming pool will be built in the town soon, and another pool is available at nearby Hillsborough River State Park.

In a park full of trees near downtown is the Alice Hall Community Center, which is the gathering point for various clubs and an assortment of civic activities.

A recent addition to the local scene is the East Pasco Medical Center, an ultra-modern facility that has 85 beds and all medical services. It opened in 1985 and is operated by the Seventh Day Adventists. Also in the field of health facilities is a city-owned nursing home with 120 beds, 60 of which are for Altzheimer patients.

Another recent arrival on the scene has been the Multi-Purpose Senior center, built in 1981. In a quiet setting among many trees on the edge of town, it serves 150 meals each noon in addition to offering bingo, dancing and classes in a variety of subjects.

Near this senior center is a city-owned airport, the only one in Pasco County. It has become a great center for parachuting and is the home of the Phoenix Parachute Center. Several meets are held there each year, and the world parachute tournament took place here in 1981.

Still another addition in the 1980s has been the city library, built in 1981. It houses 16,000 volumes plus another 15,000 paperbacks.

Zephyrhills has become the most aggressive annexer in Pasco County, having taken in over 600 acres in 1988 and planning to add more. This will help the city control its immediate surroundings and prevent still more mobile home parks being built there. It's no secret that the parks create some taxation problems because Florida's $25,000 homestead exemption law lets many owners of these mobile homes escape paying any real estate taxes.

Even with the annexation of land, there are no grandiose plans for expansion in the near future. Though the population may climb to 12,000 by 2000, the growth takes place mostly in areas outside the city and is not expected to greatly disrupt the quiet life-style Zephyrhills now enjoys.

7. SOUTH CENTRAL

Avon Park

Population 9,000. South Central. Not close to any major city. Mile-long mall in business district. Community college. Large hospital. Citrus and dairying are major industries. Part of Florida Main Street program.

The town refers to itself as the "City of Charm," and it has grown up around the mall. Running the entire length of the business district the mall is unique in that there are over a thousand varieties of trees, flowers and shrubs planted there.

Just a few miles north of Sebring in Highlands County on U.S. 27, Avon Park is another of those Florida towns with an abundance of lakes, rolling hills and citrus groves. With an elevation of 145 feet, it's part of what is referred to as the Ridge section of the state.

While the permanent population now is about 9,000, Avon Park has come a long way from a meager beginning in 1881 when Marvin Crosby arrived to start a town with a quieter kind of life. Boomtowns were springing up all over Florida then, but with them came dance halls, saloons and pollution. Crosby didn't want any of that and set about creating a town in the midst of thick pine forests.

By 1885 the first white woman arrived here. Her name was Mary King, and she had come from England with her husband. Her hometown had been Stratford-on-Avon, famous as the birthplace of William Shakespeare. And that's how Avon Park acquired its name.

Crosby fared well with his new town until a devastating freeze hit in 1895 and wiped out every citrus tree in the state.

Most people deserted the town, though Mrs. King and a few others stayed on. Avon Park gradually rebounded and was incorporated in 1926.

Somewhat isolated from the major cities of the state, the town seems to enjoy being tucked away among the orange groves. There's no night life, no big shopping malls, just a relaxed atmosphere. The people are friendly and decidedly laid-back. They don't rush to get things done today; there's always tomorrow or the day after that. Orlando and its Disney World are 78 miles away, while Tampa and Miami are 82 miles and 174 miles, respectively.

Despite the lack of hustle and bustle, Avon Park has much going for it. Agriculture dominates the scene here with citrus as king. Dairy farming also is a major industry along with sod production. Included in the latter is a special strain of turf that is well suited for athletic fields and golf courses. After miles and miles of the citrus groves, it comes as something of a surprise to see the cattle grazing alongside the highway. There's some light industry in town. Wellcraft Marine has 200 employees, while another boat manufacturer plans to hire about 500.

The largest employer in the area is Walker Memorial Hospital with a payroll of 500. A U.S. Air Force bombing range outside town has 200 men stationed there, and also nearby are a state correctional institution and an alcohol rehabilitation center, which also provide employment for Avon Park residents. From 1988 through 1990, Highlands County is expected to lead the state in job creation with an increase of 24.5 percent.

Retirees make up about a third of the 9,000 permanent population, and there are many more here in the winter. The count jumps to 14,000 then. For the older generation there's no lack of activity. A Winter Guest Club has operated on the Main Street Mall for 50 years on behalf of those winter visitors and offers card parties, suppers and other social events. There also are 24 lighted shuffleboard courts. The New Hope Senior Center, next to the town library, offers various classes and meals.

Here since 1922, the library is open six days a week and has 17,000 volumes. It's part of the county library system, so it's possible to get books and periodicals from other libraries in the county.

Recreation is a major consideration in Avon Park. There are 30 lakes within a three-mile radius of the town, and all of them are well stocked with fish. Most also have public boat ramps. For swimmers, there's a sandy beach open to the public at Donaldson Park just off Main Street.

Golfers have their choice of three courses, and there are lighted tennis courts in Donaldson Park. Heavy emphasis is placed on baseball, from the Little Leagues through high school. The local high school baseball team has won eight state championships, and several players from here have made it to the big leagues.

In 1988, Avon Park was selected for the Florida Main Street program, and this has stirred considerable interest in improving the town. There are plans for a major upgrading of stores on the mall, plus a hotel renovation project there that is decidedly unique.

The three-story Jacaranda Hotel, built in 1926 and catering largely to winter visitors, has been showing its age for several years. In a massive effort all the rooms will be redone and new shops installed on the ground floor. Tied in with this renovation is a program initiated by the South Florida Community College. The school is offering a hotel management course for 75 students who will live in a special dormitory in the hotel, attend classes there and learn first-hand how to run a hotel.

Started in the early 70s, the community college is located on an 86-acre campus a mile from Avon Park. It offers a wide range of courses, many of them technical in nature and tailored to local industries, including engineering, job printing, warehousing and computers. Those interested in adult education and night classes may choose from a long list of subjects.

The addition of the college also brought a welcome infusion of culture to the Avon Park community. Included in the series of entertainment offerings last season were productions of *Hamlet* and *The Pirates of Penzance*, the Montovani Orchestra, *Swan Lake* Ballet and Burl Ives. All are staged in a 1,500-

seat auditorium. For those interested in either seeing or participating in other stage shows, the Highlands Little Theater is only a short drive away in Sebring. Local arts groups also take part in the Sebring program.

Like so many other Florida towns, Avon Park also utilized its abandoned Seaboard Railroad station for a museum, and it opened in 1980 with an impressive display of memorabilia from the early days. The town marked its centennial in 1985.

Real estate prices are not out of line. The average selling price for a three-bedroom home is $52,000, and a four-bedroom home runs about $60,000. The county tax millage rate is $13.89, while the city is $7.65.

The aforementioned Walker Memorial Hospital is one of the town's leading assets. It's 40 years old, has 122 beds, full surgical and medical services and is the only obstetrical facility in the county.

With one of the world's great auto races just a few miles away in Sebring, it seems quite a contrast from the early days when pioneer settlers took a train from Jacksonville to Fort Meade and then rode the stagecoach to Avon Park. The pace is slightly faster now, but there's still time to relax and enjoy life in this quiet setting.

Lake Placid

Population 1,014. South Central. Not near any large cities. Major retirement center. Citrus dominates. 27 lakes in town and nearby. Fishing, sailing popular. Rowing regatta. New high school. Small hospital.

Only one town can refer to itself as "The Caladium Capital of the World," and that's Lake Placid. A whopping 80 percent of all the caladium bulbs on earth come from this little town in south central Florida.

Mention of Lake Placid usually stirs thoughts of the Winter Olympics as they were twice held in that New York village. While the Lake Placid in Florida has some imposing hills and all kinds of lakes, the climate would not be suitable for winter sports. There's no snow for skiing on the hills, and the lakes never freeze over for ice skating.

This more southerly Lake Placid does have a tie, though, with its namesake up north. Back in 1927, Dr. Melvin Dewey, originator of the Dewey Decimal System, his wife and other members of the Lake Placid Club had visions of establishing a resort town here which would surpass theirs in New York. The group talked city officials into changing the town's name to Lake Placid, and it stuck.

In the more than 60 years since, many changes have taken place. There are still only 1,014 people living in the Lake Placid city limits, but there are another 24,000 residents in the surrounding area, all with a Lake Placid mailing address.

This little town really jumps out as you approach it through thousands of acres of orange trees and lakes on all sides. There are 27 lakes within the city and many more in the area.

Orange groves, lakes and rolling hills mark the landscape around Lake Placid, "The Caladium Capital of the World."

The housing developments outside the city are visible up and down the hills in every direction. U.S. Highway 27 skirted the original business district of Lake Placid, and the big supermarkets and chains have sprung up along the highway. The older small stores are still downtown, along with the schools and much of the town's activities.

Many retirees have found their way to this somewhat isolated spot in the southern part of the Florida peninsula. About a third of those living in Lake Placid and the adjoining area are retirees, mostly from the northeast. Young adults too have been relocating to Lake Placid to raise their families and take advantage of the open spaces, new schools and a rapidly developing economy.

Agriculture is the dominating force, and citrus is the king. There are 215 citrus growers in Highlands County, and Lake Placid is the southernmost town. These growers recently produced 12.5 million boxes in a single season, worth $60 million. Other important agricultural pursuits include truck farming, cattle ranching and horticulture research. The town is also special in having one of the few pineapple farms in the state. And then there are the caladiums. There are 27 farms exclusively devoted to raising these variably-colored plants that are shipped all over the world from Lake Placid.

While Lake Placid didn't add much population in large numbers until U.S. 27 pushed down here in the early 50s, the town's history goes back to the earliest years of this century. It is located on the land set aside for the Seminole Nation in 1842. In 1909 Congress opened the lands for homesteading, and by 1912 there were 75 homesteaders here. The railroad arrived in 1917. The town was known at various times as Lake Buck, Lake June, Lake Stearns and Wicco until the folks from New York got it changed.

Despite all the agriculture and industry, there's plenty of time devoted to recreation and a wealth of facilities. There are three public golf courses in town, two with 18 holes and one with nine holes. There are lighted tennis courts, a swimming pool that's open in the summer, four lighted ball fields, a skating rink and shuffleboard courts. The latter are at the Tourist Club, which also has a building for card players.

Much of the area's recreation, though, is centered on the water in those 27 lakes. For the fishermen and boaters, this is the place to be. Most of the local lakes have boat ramps, and there are tournaments held year-round by the Lake Placid Bassers Fishing Club. Bass weighing six to eight pounds are pulled out regularly, and there are plenty of panfish. Water skiing and swimming in these lakes are enjoyed in all months.

Sailing is a major sport in Lake Placid, thanks largely to Florida's Lake Country Yacht Club, which has a busy schedule of activities. It starts in April with "Take Friday Off," the first spring sailing series of races, and it's still going with the fall series of races in November. The club also sponsors a rowing regatta in June that attracts entries from all over Florida.

With the recent influx of new residents has come a huge expansion of the school system in Lake Placid. A new high school complex was recently built at a cost of $3 million, while new middle and elementary schools are being built at a cost of $7 million.

Many of the local students go to a satellite campus of South Florida Community College for a couple more years of education after high school. Adult classes also are offered.

A somewhat small library is now being doubled in size, and its current inventory of 9,600 volumes will be increased when the construction is finished.

A town of this size doesn't usually have a hospital, but this one is spending $3 million for an expansion to the Lake Placid Medical Center that will add 50 beds and provide full services. Large medical centers also are available at Sebring and Avon Park in the same county.

The real estate market is reasonable. There are good homes with two or three bedrooms for less than $50,000. Ones of that size on a lake with a sandy beach are available for under $100,000. The Lake Placid tax millage rate is $19.01.

An elevator takes visitors to the top of Placid Tower, the town's leading tourist attraction. It rises 270 feet from the ground and was the world's largest concrete masonry structure when it was built in 1960. There's no lack of events scheduled through the year. The Lake Placid Art League holds its annual art show in January. A month later there's the annual Arts and Crafts Country Fair, followed by the Historical Society's Pioneer Week. On Memorial Day there's the Orange Crate Derby, patterned after the Soap Box Derby, with all of the carts being made by local students.

The Historical Society also has been active in renovating an abandoned railroad depot for a museum that has three rooms full of exhibits, including a red caboose.

Those looking for cultural events have an outstanding dinner theater in nearby Sebring and the cultural series offered each year at South Florida Community College in Avon Park.

In many ways Lake Placid has most of the amenities of city life while still enjoying its small town charm. There aren't too many towns quite like this one.

Sebring

Population 9,500. South Central. Not close to any large cities. Major citrus producing area. Outstanding Cultural Center. Large library, will expand. Site of important auto race in spring. Hospital. State park nearby.

Folks in Florida think of Sebring as one of the state's prettiest towns. For those outside Florida, it's usually known as the site of one of the world's greatest auto races.

This is a town that has just about everything on the plus side. Nestled among the rolling hills of south central Florida, it's surrounded by lush orange groves, thousands of palm trees and towering pines. Sebring's population is about 10,000, and it has not experienced any spectacular growth. This figure doubles in the winter, and another 33,000 live in close proximity outside the city limits.

The town was founded by George Sebring in 1912. A ceramic manufacturer in Ohio, Sebring moved here to create a new town in a wilderness. He selected a small oak tree to be the center with all roads radiating from there. A road was built around the oak tree, and the businesses, many still there, were built on this circle. All other streets spread out from that circle in a unique arrangement to form the downtown area. Now a picturesque little park has been built at the spot where Sebring started his town.

Sebring grew quickly and jumped from 800 population to 7,000 between 1920 and 1926. Then the Florida boom collapsed, and the figure had dropped to 3,500 by 1930. It had started its recovery by the advent of World War II, when a training base for B-17s was built there. When U.S. Highway 27 was built in the early 50s, the town was readily accessible, and the population quickly accelerated.

Host to one of the world's greatest auto races, Sebring also boasts an impressive cultural center complex with revolving theater.

That old air base became the site of the 12 Hours of Sebring in 1952, and now crowds of more than 50,000 auto racing fans pour into this little Florida city annually. The race is second only to Indianapolis in international significance.

Half of the permanent population is composed of retirees, most of whom moved here from the northeast and Midwest, plus the coastal areas of Florida. The latter blame traffic, congestion and crime as the reasons for moving to Sebring.

People on the street say the town's a good place to raise a family, and crime is almost nonexistent. Everyone seems friendly, and the pace is definitely on the slow side. It's 162 miles to Miami, 86 to Orlando and 90 to Tampa.

Real estate prices are reasonable. Homes with two bedrooms and two baths are available for under $50,000, and some new three-bedroom homes are being offered for under $40,000. The millage rate is $22.11.

Lake Jackson, which is entirely surrounded by Sebring, is the water recreation center of the town. It's 11 miles in radius, has three public beaches, public boat ramps and a public pier for fishing. The water is clear, and there's always a lot of activity there. Scenic Lakeview Drive encircles the lake.

There's a wealth of other recreation facilities, including 22 tennis courts, seven golf courses, a public swimming pool, 36 shuffleboard courts, two racquetball courts, two softball fields and three lighted baseball fields for the various youth programs.

For nature lovers, Highlands Hammock State Park just a few miles outside Sebring is the oldest state park in Florida. Many of its trees are thought to be almost 1,000 years old.

On Lake Jackson, just a short distance from downtown, is an attractive Cultural Center complex unmatched by most larger cities. A modernistic library has 37,000 volumes and will have a large addition in 1990. A few feet from the library is the Highlands Little Theater—a dinner theater now seating 192 after a recent enlargement that included a revolving stage. The price for a show and prime rib dinner is only $19.50, and the five offerings during the recent season were *Cabaret, Barefoot in the Park, Carousel, California Suite* and *Damn Yankees*. Built for the USO during the war, the theater's new stage is as large as several on Broadway.

Rounding out this complex is a new art museum and a civic center. The art museum is open daily and displays works of local artists, while the civic center is used for meetings and various other activities. The main industries in Sebring are citrus, tourism and winter vegetable crops. Lesco, a lawn mower manufacturer, is a major industry with 200 employees.

Highlands County, of which Sebring is the county seat, boasts of a progressive school system that includes South Florida Community College at nearby Avon Park. Adult education classes are offered there.

Sebring became a member of the Florida Main Street program in 1986 and has made important strides in improving its downtown business section. Like most Florida cities, the large stores and supermarkets have moved to the edge of the city, in Sebring's case to U.S. 27. Specialty shops, some 75 years old, are downtown.

The park where George Sebring started it all and the adjacent business blocks were refurbished in 1985. Lights which had been there 30 years ago were recovered from the city dump. They were multi-bulb lamps which were the first electric lights installed in Sebring in 1914. Of the original 12, nine were restorable. Benches, in the park since 1925 and relegated to the city barn 30 years ago, were also brought back and restored.

Medical facilities in the county are among the best in Florida. In Sebring, Highlands Regional Medical center, with 126 beds, recently spent $6.5 million in renovation and a major addition. At Avon Park, Walker Memorial is another large and modern facility.

While the 12-hour auto race in March is the biggest event of the year, other outstanding activities take place. Each May a large downtown festival called the Roaring Twenties Day features merchants dressed in clothes of that era who offer some items with 1920s prices. The entertainment includes cloggers, musicians, a caladium sale, art fair and vintage car show. In November the Highlands Art League sponsors its annual art festival, one of the top rated shows in Florida. It's been held for over 20 years and attracts about 230 artists from all parts of the U.S. In February, a month before the 12 Hours of Sebring race, the Highlands County Fair is held.

Getting to Sebring is not a problem. In addition to being on four-laned U.S. 27, the city has Amtrak service, and the local airport now has two concrete runways of 5,000 feet each.

Immediately outside the city there are several housing developments, and there probably will be more as the area continues to attract retirees and younger people from the coastal areas of Florida. There are nine square miles of Sebring, but there are no plans for any expansion.

Back in the early years after George Sebring got the town started, small children used to amuse themselves by riding up Center Street in little carts pulled by giant turtles. That seems like a long time ago. The pace isn't quite that slow now, but it's also not as fast as those sports cars which zoom around the race course each March.

There's a good mix of retirees and young people, a good mix of tourism and industry and a life-style that the town appears bent on protecting. Very few Florida towns of this size have come up with so many pluses.

8. SOUTHWEST

North Port

Population 9,800. Southwest. Midway between Sarasota and Fort Myers, near gulf. New town, started in 1959. Many retirees. Good recreational facilities, cultural activities. Senior Center. Branch of community college.

It's the third largest city in Florida in area, yet only a small percentage of the state's population has ever heard of North Port.

Near the gulf and a network of canals, North Port offers boating enthusiasts facilities for all types of craft.

Here is a town of almost 10,000 in Sarasota County that was total wilderness until the late 1950s, when the Mackle brothers started developing the area. By 1970, the population was only 2,244, but the word has gotten out since, and more retirees and others are now finding their way to North Port.

Located halfway between Fort Myers and Sarasota in southwest Florida and only a few miles from the Gulf of Mexico, North Port is a town of 76 square miles. Only five percent of those 76 square miles have been developed, but 90,000 homesites have been platted.

The town was incorporated in 1959 when there were only 10 families in North Port, and all of them worked for the Mackles. In the 30 years since, the place has become something of a model community with all the amenities that some towns spend almost a century achieving. The Mackles are no longer involved in developing it.

About 40 percent of the population is 65 or over, so considerable attention has been devoted to providing the facilities that folks in that age bracket want for their retirement years. The working people who make up the balance of the population generally commute to jobs in Fort Myers, Venice, Port Charlotte or Punta Gorda.

While almost all of the better towns in Florida still have a few blocks of slums or unsightly sections, North Port has none. The most common size home in town has two bedrooms and two baths in about 1,400 square feet and sells for an average price between $50,000 and $60,000. The most expensive houses are those fronting on a canal or the golf course. Two and three-bedroom homes rent for $325 to $400 a month.

North Port has a very short history. Only 30 years old, the town can't regale visitors with tales of Spanish explorers, wars with hostile Indians or Victorian houses. Everything in North Port is late 20th century, except for some remarkable findings of divers in the 1950s. These fellows and others since found in a large hole well-preserved botanical and human remains deposited as long as 10,000 years ago at the end of the ice age. The 220-foot hole just north of North Port city limits has yielded such a rare collection of artifacts that it has been placed on the National Register of Historic Places.

Those who move to Florida to spend much of their time outdoors will find North Port an ideal place to live. The facilities are many and excellent.

Most of the residents like the idea of fishing on a year-round basis, and in this town they can take their choice of fresh water or salt water. North Port has a large network of fresh water canals, and those looking for this type of fishing will be rewarded with catches of bass that range between two and 12 pounds, along with bluegill, bream, speckled perch and catfish in the area creeks. Deep-sea enthusiasts have easy access to the gulf through Charlotte Harbor and bring in king or Spanish mackerel, grouper, redfish and snapper. They also find a challenge in the tarpon, a very bony inedible fish that is an exciting adversary. Those favoring snook head for the Myakka River or Myakkahatchee Creek.

Many residents own boats. These range from canoes and rowboats that are perfect for the winding creeks and streams north of U.S. Highway 41 in North Port to yachts and power boats. So many have yachts that a large North Port Yacht Club is active with its own building on the edge of town. The canoeists have a launch spot near the parking lot at the North Port Community Park.

For recreation facilities, the residents have a choice of 12 parks of varying sizes scattered through the town. Among the facilities are three lighted handball courts, several lighted tennis courts, 10 shuffleboard courts, a Little League field, softball field, baseball field for seniors, two soccer fields, two basketball courts, volleyball courts and horseshoe pits.

In a well-kept athletic complex in Dallas White Park is a large swimming pool that's open 360 days of the year. In addition there are bicycle trails and wilderness and jogging trails throughout the town on both sides of U.S. 41 and plenty of playground equipment for the younger generation. The golfers have an 18-hole layout that is semi-private and has water on every hole. Those wishing to swim in the gulf will find superb beaches at Englewood, 12 miles away.

Cultural activities include a North Port Concert Orchestra, composed of strictly local talent, which presents four concerts a year in the Presbyterian church. About 25 to 30 members of this orchestra have organized a brass band that performs almost every Thursday night in the North Port Mall. A chorale group also schedules two concerts each season, and an art guild got started in 1988. In Sarasota, just 35 miles away, there are programs ranging from jazz to opera, ballet to contemporary dance and experimental theater to Broadway musicals.

The town doesn't have a hospital, but there are excellent medical facilities that include a walk-in clinic, an X-ray lab and a 100-bed convalescent center that opened in 1985. the nearest hospitals are in Port Charlotte and Venice, a few minutes away by ambulance. There are 12 physicians and three dentists in town.

Another plus for the health conscious is located just north of the city limits at one of the world's greatest health spas, Natural Warm Springs. The water here at a constant 87 degrees attracts thousands each year who seek relief from muscular problems, arthritis and rheumatism.

In recent years the city has built an impressive senior center. This center goes a step beyond the usual program of Meals on Wheels by offering candlelight dinners every Tuesday through Friday night. Other programs there include ballroom dancing, bridge, pinochle, jazzercise, Spanish classes, a Singleton Club, basic exercise and AARP meetings.

The town doesn't have a high school, but an elementary school for 700 children was built in 1984, and a middle school is planned for 1990. Buses take the high school kids to Venice.

North Port citizens interested in furthering their education don't have far to go. A branch of Manatee Community College operates just west of North Port in a secluded area on U.S. 41. The school places heavy emphasis on high tech and computer sciences and also is training students in laser technology, telemetry and robotics.

In the spring local residents are only seven miles from the training base of the Texas Rangers in Port Charlotte. They catch the exhibition games then and have 70 more to watch when a Florida State League team plays there during the summer.

Shopping facilities in town include two large shopping centers and a large mall, all along U.S. 41. A regional mall is scheduled to open soon in the nearby town of Murdock.

Since the early 60s the town has had its own tourist attraction, the American Police Hall of Fame and Museum. Located along the highway, the building contains collections of photographs, artifacts and weapons concerning law enforcement officers, criminals and victims. There's also a memorial listing all U.S. police officers killed in the line of duty since 1960. It's open daily for a small admission fee.

North Port is a well-planned city. In addition to fully staffed police and fire departments, a well-designed city hall includes a large room for council meetings and more seating for the public than some larger cities can offer.

The tax rates are not out of line. The millage is $5.67 in the city and $11.98 in the county.

Among the many other amenities are a public library with 26,000 books that is open six days a week, 26 churches and a community center used for meetings by the more than 75 clubs operating in the community. It's worth noting that many of the public buildings and park facilities have been built by private donations.

Several events are held each year in North Port. These include an azalea sale in the spring, a poinsettia parade at Christmas and the North Port Days. The latter is held during February and March and features concerts, art and photography shows, a Kiwanis pancake breakfast and a walkathon for all ages to raise scholarship funds for local students.

Just 12 miles away in Venice, the Ringling Circus has had its winter quarters since 1960 and puts on its premier show each year before starting its travels through the north.

For a town that was carved out of the wilderness in such a relatively short time, North Port has much to recommend it. The place is certain to grow in the years ahead, but it seems unlikely it will experience one of those population explosions that have hit so many other Florida communities. Up to now the town has been a well-kept secret, even among most Floridians. Until the rest of the state becomes aware of it, North Port will probably continue to enjoy the good life and not have to contend with any mass migrations here.

Punta Gorda

Population 9,500. Southwest. 24 miles north of Fort Myers. Heavy growth in area in recent years. Citrus, commercial fishing major industries. Good recreational facilities. Large hospital, good library. Annual air show.

One of the great ironies of Florida is that it was the first part of the U.S. to be discovered by white men and the last to be fully settled.

In the area where Punta Gorda is located, the earliest Spanish explorers are believed to have made their landings. Now, more than 400 years later, Punta Gorda has developed into one of the busiest towns on Florida's southwest coast and one of the most popular places to live. It's the county seat of Charlotte County and the only incorporated town in the county. The population in 1988 was 9,500, but this figure doubles when the snowbirds arrive in the winter, mostly from the Midwest.

This area is rich in history. A settlement on Charlotte Harbor, where Punta Gorda is situated, was established by Juan Ponce de Leon in 1522, a century before the Pilgrims landed on Plymouth Rock and a quarter century before St. Augustine was founded. Just 17 years later, Hernando de Soto is believed to have landed in the same harbor and camped at a place now called Live Oak Point.

Both of these famous explorers met tragic fates in the New World. Ponce de Leon's settlement at Punta Gorda consisted of a band of 200 soldiers, priests, farmers, artisans and monks. Their colony lasted only six months, collapsing after a battle with Caloosa Indians in which Ponce de Leon was mortally wounded. He was taken to Havana and died there. The fate of de Soto was no better. He sailed from Spain in 1538, stopped in Cuba, landed near Punta Gorda and then spent nearly four years exploring Florida and the territory that now comprises eight other states. In 1542, a fever killed de Soto

A center for golf, tennis, yachting, Punta Gorda sponsors an international air show and wind surfing competition.

in what is now the state of Mississippi, and he was buried in the Mississippi River.

Over 300 years would elapse from those early explorations before Punta Gorda was formed. The town was platted by Isaac Trabue on February 24, 1885. More than two years later a group of men decided the community should be incorporated, filing the necessary papers on December 7, 1887. Trabue was the original name of the town but was soon changed to Punta Gorda, a Spanish translation for broad point. Spanish fishermen had first given it that name in the early 1800s.

The early days of the town were not impressive. As recently as the early 1920s, the council met in a poolroom or a store, and the town was little more than a fishing village. By 1924, the city hall, still in use, was built, and Punta Gorda began to share in the Florida boom of the following years.

To realize the terrific growth that has hit this area in the years since World War II, it should be noted that the population of Punta Gorda in 1950 was only 1,915, and the head count for Charlotte County was just 4,286. In 1988, these figures had skyrocketed to 9,500 and 88,000.

Fortunately for Punta Gorda the growth has been well monitored. There are strict zoning regulations, and the residents and town officials have planned well for development. Directly across from Charlotte Harbor is the growing city of Port Charlotte, an unincorporated place of more than 50,000.

Charlotte County didn't exist until 1920, when it was formed from part of DeSoto County. Punta Gorda became the county seat that year, and there were only 500 voters in the county. The courthouse was built six years later.

In the downtown section a revitalization committee is engaged in fixing up the old portion of the business district with new store fronts and replanting the royal palm trees. These stately trees, found only in south Florida, were originally planted by Albert Gilchrist in 1900. This gentleman later became governor of Florida and also is remembered for an unusual provision in his will. He stipulated that $5,000 be set aside with the interest from that amount being used each year to buy candy for the children of Punta Gorda at Halloween. The candy was later changed to ice cream, and last year the

$5,000 earned $300 to supply 1,200 ice cream bars for the small fry. Adjacent to the downtown area are many charming older homes that also are undergoing restoration.

Single family homes predominate in Punta Gorda, though there are several condos and four mobile home parks in town. Prices range from $40,500 and up for two and three-bedroom single family homes. Residential lots of a quarter acre are about $3,500. For those wanting homes on a canal or on the harbor, the prices accelerate in a hurry. A lot on a canal, and there are 110 miles of canals in Punta Gorda, will cost $17,000 and up. Homes in these areas are all in six figures, and some are close to $500,000. Punta Gorda Isles, directly on the harbor, is the costliest area in town.

Taxes, despite all the amenities, are not excessive, and the Punta Gorda millage rate is only $3.40. The cost of living here ranks 38th of Florida's 67 counties.

With so much water around, it's not surprising that the most popular sports are centered here. The Peace River, which flows into Charlotte Harbor, is heavily used for fishing, boating and camping. A large yacht club is active at Punta Gorda Isles, where Fishermen's Village, built to resemble the original, has an impressive shopping mall of fancy shops and restaurants. For the hunters, the C.M. Webb Wildlife Management Area of 65,000 acres is open for hunting and has a wealth of small game, despite the encroaching civilization.

The golfers have their choice of two private and two semi-private courses. At Gilchrist Park there are four tennis courts, plus volleyball and shuffleboard courts, all lighted. There are three more tennis courts and two racquetball courts at the junior high. Softball and baseball facilities are located in the parks, and there's also a jogging trail and public pool.

While Punta Gorda has only small industries now, more than 3,000 acres have been set aside for an industrial park. The largest employer is Mec-O-Matic, which makes controls for pumps and employs over 100 people.

Despite all the growth, there's still plenty of space outside Punta Gorda for agriculture. Over 7,400 acres are planted in oranges and another 500 acres in grapefruit. These groves produce over two million boxes of fruit each year. Vegetables also are an important crop with 1,195 acres of them planted. There are 29,000 head of cattle in the county, and most of them are on the 90,000 acre Babcock Ranch east of town on U.S. Highway 17. That ranch also raises alligators and ostriches. Commercial fishing also is an important part of the economy, producing over four million pounds of food fish in a year.

Cultural activities play a major role in the life of Punta Gorda. The Memorial Auditorium had a busy schedule in a recent season that included the Guy Lombardo, Myron Floren and Russ Morgan Orchestras, Sid Caesar, Charley Pride, Mel Torme and George Shearing, the Preservation Hall Jazz Band, Mantovani and Roger Williams, plus productions of *Cabaret*, *Sweet Charity* and *Sugar Babies*.

An Art Guild has been active for 27 years, and a Visual Art Center is under construction. The Babcock Ranch donated $250,000 toward this project.

Across the harbor the Charlotte Chamber Orchestra has performed for over ten seasons and brings in noted guest artists. There's also a little theater group there, the Port Charlotte Players.

The Punta Gorda library is an attractive building with over 30,000 volumes.

There's no shortage of special events in town. A re-enactment of Ponce de Leon's landing with his conquistadores is held on the shores of Charlotte Harbor in February, along with a fishing tournament in March and April, a two-day Florida International Air Show in the spring that is among the five largest in the U.S. and a wind surfing regatta in October. The Texas Rangers train each spring at Port Charlotte.

Punta Gorda has three elementary schools, a junior high school and a senior high school. The Charlotte Vocational-Technical Center is considered the best in Florida and has been responsible for attracting some of the existing industries to Punta Gorda. Edison Community College has a branch in Port Charlotte, as does Florida Southern College, a four-year institution. Adult education courses are available at all of these.

Medical facilities include the Medical Center Hospital in

Punta Gorda that's run by the Seventh Day Adventists and has 208 beds plus a cancer unit and cardiac care. There are two other large hospitals elsewhere in the county and five licensed nursing homes.

Retirees have been a major factor in the area's growth. The county has the highest median age of any county in the U.S., and 54 percent of the residents are over 55.

Even with this growth, though, there are still reminders around of Punta Gorda's earliest days. An ice house that was built in 1898 and made Punta Gorda a commercial center then is still standing. A major street through town is named Burnt Store Road, and the history of that goes back to the 1850s, when a man named Kennedy established a trading post on Charlotte Harbor. During the third Seminole War the Indians burned down the store, hence Burnt Store Road.

That people will continue moving into Punta Gorda seems a certainty. Its status as a small town may be in jeopardy, and there already are predictions of the population doubling by 2000. Many folks already are moving here from Fort Myers, 24 miles away, because of the lower prices. Crowded as it is, though, on that broad point of land for which it was named, Punta Gorda is not likely to change in character. Any large growth in the future will have to be east of the town, and that is comforting to those who are already settled here.

About the Author

A native of Nashua, Iowa, Bob Howard retired in 1987 after 41 years in the newspaper business. All but five of those years were spent with the *Orlando Sentinel*, where he served at different times as sports editor, executive editor, assistant to the publisher and public services manager.

Howard is a graduate of Cornell College in Iowa and spent three years during World War II with the U.S. Navy, most of it in Pearl Harbor. He's married and has three daughters.

An avid bicyclist, the author rode 4,600 miles across the U.S., from Seattle to Bar Harbor, Maine, shortly after turning 65 and retiring. He continues to bicycle at least 20 miles daily.

Since moving to Orlando in 1951, Howard has toured the state extensively and traveled hundreds of miles in accumulating the information used to determine the best small towns in the state. Though he has lived in the Orlando metropolitan area throughout his years in Florida, he still feels the best living in the state is in the small towns.

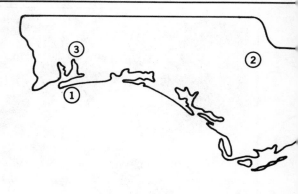

1. Gulf Breeze	**19.** Lake Wales
2. Marianna	**20.** Mount Dora
3. Milton	**21.** Orange City
4. Live Oak	**22.** St. Cloud
5. Madison	**23.** Tavares
6. Monticello	**24.** Brooksville
7. Alachua	**25.** Cedar Key
8. Belleview	**26.** Crystal River
9. Crescent City	**27.** Dade City
10. McIntosh	**28.** Dunnellon
11. Trenton	**29.** Inverness
12. Micanopy	**30.** Zephyrhills
13. Fernandina Beach	**31.** Avon Park
14. Auburndale	**32.** Lake Placid
15. Clermont	**33.** Sebring
16. DeBary	**34.** North Port
17. Eustis	**35.** Punta Gorda
18. Frostproof	

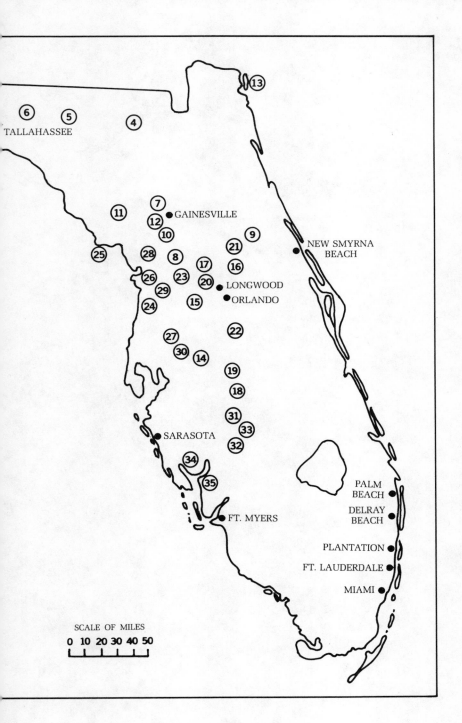

TALLAHASSEE

⑥ ⑤ ④

⑦ ● GAINESVILLE
⑪ ⑫
⑩
⑨
⑳
⑧ ㉑
㉕ ㉘ ⑰ ⑯
㉖ ㉓ ⑳ ● LONGWOOD
㉙ ● ORLANDO
㉔ ⑮
㉒
㉗
㉚ ⑭
⑲
⑱
㉛
㉝
㉜

● NEW SMYRNA
BEACH

● SARASOTA

㉞
㉟

● FT. MYERS

⑬

PALM
BEACH ●
DELRAY
BEACH ●

PLANTATION ●
FT. LAUDERDALE ●

MIAMI ●

SCALE OF MILES
0 10 20 30 40 50